GABRIEL MIRO

Nuestro Padre San Daniel
and El obispo leproso

C. A. Longhurst

Professor of Spanish
University of Exeter

Grant & Cutler Ltd
in association with Tamesis Books Ltd

ISBN 0 7293 0354 3

I.S.B.N. 84-599-3365-2

DEPÓSITO LEGAL: V. 265-1994

Printed in Spain by
Artes Gráficas Soler, S.A., Valencia
for
GRANT & CUTLER LTD
55-57 GREAT MARLBOROUGH STREET, LONDON W1V 2AY

1 00 020599 2

Critical Guides to Spanish Texts

58 Miró: Nuestro Padre San Daniel *and* El obispo leproso

Critical Guides to Spanish Texts

EDITED BY J.E. VAREY, A.D. DEYERMOND AND C.DAVIES

Contents

Prefatory Note

References to the text of *Nuestro Padre San Daniel* and *El obispo leproso* are to the edition prepared by Carlos Ruiz Silva and published by Ediciones de la Torre in 1981 and 1984 respectively. The two volumes are referred to as I and II and are followed by the appropriate page number. The figures in italic type refer to the numbered items in the Bibliographical Note; where appropriate, the italicized figures are followed by page numbers.

I should like to take this opportunity of recording my grateful thanks to Professor Ian Macdonald of Aberdeen University for bibliographical help unstintingly given; to the Inter-Library Loan Service of the University of Exeter for dealing patiently and efficiently with my many requests; and to Jennie for unfailingly answering my call for proof readers without resorting to the divorce courts.

1. The Oleza Novels: Composition, Structure, and Development

Nuestro Padre San Daniel and *El obispo leproso*, known jointly as the Oleza novels, are without the slightest doubt Miró's crowning achievement as a novelist and one of the truly outstanding works of fiction of modern Spain. Published in 1921 and 1926 respectively, these two volumes earned Miró both admiration from those who recognized the extraordinary qualities of his writing, and abuse from those who saw his work as decadent in manner and content. The fierce polemics which developed in the Spanish press following the publication of *El obispo leproso* have obscured the real points at issue in Miró's work and may even have retarded the scholarly study of his novels. The last two decades, however, have seen an enormous advance in our knowledge of this writer, with the appearance of books and articles on the sources and the art of Miró which have both increased our appreciation of his skills and brought about a renaissance of his reputation as writer and novelist. The aim of this Critical Guide is starkly simple: to offer a comment upon those aspects of the Oleza novels that have seemed particularly important, and to guide the reader of Miró through a work of literature which, although difficult to the new reader, greatly rewards close attention.

One immediate difficulty with Miró is the extraordinary richness of his vocabulary: unusual words abound and demand frequent use of the dictionary. Another is the equally extraordinary range of his literary references, particularly to religious texts. This Critical Guide addresses neither of those difficulties, for the purely practical reason of space. But in any case there are now available scholarly and helpful editions of the Oleza novels in which the editors have solved virtually all the linguistic and allusive problems and obscurities (*30, 31, 29, 36*).

Nuestro Padre San Daniel and *El obispo leproso* appear to have had a long gestation, since Miró's references to a work with 'obispo leproso' as part of the title go back to 1912. In fact the idea may have come to him even earlier, for his association with leprosy dates from 1902, when he visited the Alicantine village of Parcent and its leper colony. This visit inspired him to write his first recognized work, the travelogue *Del vivir* (1904; he repudiated two earlier works). *Del vivir*, half-fact, half-fiction, or perhaps better described as fact transformed by the techniques of fiction, is precisely about the social isolation and mental suffering of the lepers and in a general sense about pain. There is therefore an obvious connection between this very early work and the much later story of the leprous bishop of Oleza. But Miró would also have had the subject suggested to him by a real-life bishop of Orihuela, the Spanish city in the province of Alicante (though closer to Murcia) on which Oleza is closely modelled. Miró may even have had two separate bishops in mind: one, Archbishop Fernando Loaces who lived in the sixteenth century, reputedly suffered from leprosy but was cured, and the other, in modern times, Bishop Juan Maura, who was bishop of Orihuela between 1886 and 1910, and who, though not a leper, did suffer from some lesser skin disease which obliged him to wear purple gloves, like Miró's fictitious character (*6*, pp.45–46).

But although the idea of a leprous bishop must have been at the root of Miró's inspiration for the work, the Oleza novels are clearly very much more than the story of a single character. Indeed the outstanding quality of the work is arguably the extraordinary breadth and richness of the personages that populate its pages, Miró's ability to create and portray characters being nothing short of remarkable. No single character dominates the work, all being in an important sense connected with and subordinated to the whole, and this whole, as we shall see, is the city of Oleza itself and the author's particular vision of that city.

Leprosy, a bishop, a city and its people: these are the basic ingredients out of which Miró built his two-volume novel. We do not know why it was so long in the writing — apart from the fact that other work, some commissioned, interrupted the slow process of composition — nor why Miró published it in two volumes. To judge from his own references to his work in his correspondence, it seems likely that parts of Volume II were written before Volume I, and that the latter may have been expanded to form a book-length volume and published under a separate and new title while completion of the second volume, with the originally-intended title, was deferred pending the satisfactory resolution of whatever problems Miró had encountered (*31*, pp.15–16).

Whatever the reason for the five-year gap in publication, the two volumes are inseparable, and Miró established very precise links between the two, as we shall see. But it is possible that certain events which occurred after he published his *Figuras de la Pasión del Señor* in 1916 and 1917 may have persuaded him to revise or expand what he had so far written in order to underscore the clerical obscurantism that still affected much of the Spanish political right. *Figuras de la Pasión del Señor* was an imaginative evocation of the final days of Christ, a subject which Miró treats, if not in an orthodox manner, at any rate respectfully and sympathetically. Yet the artistic transformation to which he subjected the Gospels aroused the ire of the clerical right, and the work was attacked as heretical and decadent, a newspaper editor who had dared to publish a chapter even being sent to jail for blasphemy (*14*, p.18). Miró was appalled that his work could be so patently misunderstood, and put it down to the ultramontane, reactionary propaganda of certain clerical circles. The subtle but devastating critique of religious bigotry in the Oleza novels may thus owe something to the clerical disparagement of *Figuras*, although predictably the attacks on Miró were to become even more pronounced and irrational after the publication of *El obispo leproso* and may even have cost him his election to the Royal Spanish Academy (*28*, p.331 and *31*, pp.63–66). Miró himself ascribed the campaign of vilification against him to behind-the-scenes manoeuvres of the Jesuits. The fact is that if with *Figuras* Miró had strayed into forbidden territory, with *El obispo leproso* he had taken on the might of a still powerful segment of Spanish society.

All this is not to say that the sole object, or even the

overriding aim, of the Oleza novels is religious satire. Miró's characters are fictitious, the storyline is fictitious, and everything is subjected to the techniques of fiction. But at the same time Miró has borrowed heavily from the real world, and the framework for the novel is, in broad terms, faithful to history. It is faithful both on a personal and on a general level: on the personal because Miró is recreating the Orihuela that he knew as a boy, when he attended the Jesuit school there between the ages of eight and thirteen; on the general because he has set the story in a clearly recognizable historical epoch and has provided a supporting structure of historical reference. It would be as mistaken to think of this work as a historical novel as it would be to dismiss the historical content as mere padding. Miró was not a theoretician of the genre, so he made scarcely any statements about his own theory or even approach to the novel. But from the few statements that can be elicited one can deduce that he believed that reality underlay everything that the artist did — either through direct observation or via memory. 'The reality behind the Oleza novels' — writes Marian Coope — 'consists of both the physical world he knew and the documentation from newspapers and histories with which he made his books' (6, p.13). This particular scholar has made an exhaustive study of the real-life sources of inspiration of Miró and has proved beyond doubt that, work of fiction though it manifestly is, the point of departure for Miró was reality itself: events, people and places had in many instances counterparts in real life, although naturally Miró has subjected his raw material to a process of transformation. In this Critical Guide we shall be concerned with the process of transformation itself, that is to say with the salient qualities of Miró's art that make the Oleza novels what they are. But first it is important to sketch in the historical background of the work.

Indirect references rather than specific dates allow us to infer that the events of the novel take place during the last two decades of the nineteenth century. Orihuela was then a provincial backwater, though that in itself made it more rather than less typical of the bulk of Spain. Whereas Madrid and the larger cities were predominantly liberal in outlook, the countryside and smaller towns were more conservative and therefore more favourable to Carlism, which still looked to Church and King for the political guidance of the country.[1] The Carlists made three attempts to defeat the Madrid government and bring about a change of dynasty by military means, all of which ended in failure, the third and last Carlist War taking place between 1872 and 1876, only a relatively short time before the events of Miró's novel. Both this aspect and the fact that Carlism had been stronger and more active in the north and east of Spain than in the west, centre or south are very clearly reflected in the Oleza novels, which are full of references to and reminiscences of the armed struggle.[2] Carlism was by now politically moribund but it still wielded considerable influence in certain social and ecclesiastical circles, since its ideology was after all based on the belief that political life should be dominated by a narrowly religious view of life. Those who shared this approach to politics would naturally tend to be Carlists rather than Liberals. Many, probably most, Liberals were devout Catholics, but were happy to see the Church and the body politic kept at arm's length from each other. The political division of Spain into Liberals and Carlists was thus much more than a simple division according to political allegiance. It was a confrontation between two opposing beliefs about the role of religion and the Church in national life and about tradition versus modernization. It is this ideological confrontation and its social consequences that Miró has sought to reflect in his novel of provincial life. Carlos Ruiz Silva sums it up in this way:

---

[1] The Carlists were the followers of Don Carlos María Isidro and his descendants. Don Carlos would have become king of Spain upon the death of his brother King Ferdinand VII in 1833 but for the fact that Ferdinand revoked the Salic Law of 1713, which prevented the accession of females to the throne, and named his daughter Isabel as successor. In order to survive, the Isabelline faction was forced to seek support from moderate Liberals. The Carlists by contrast gained the support of the most conservative elements of Spanish society.

[2] For an identification and explanation of all the historical references to Carlism in the Oleza novels see Marian Coope (6, pp.110–23).

> Lo importante para el escritor es ofrecer la esencia de
> una ciudad...de provincias, de Levante, con todo su
> trasfondo histórico y social: el poder de la Iglesia, la
> lucha entre la mentalidad ultraconservadora — carlista
> en este caso — y la liberal, la diferencia y relación entre
> sus clases sociales, la dificultad — o imposibilidad —
> de la realización personal en un ambiente carente de
> libertad. Lo que Miró identifica en su novela con la
> realidad no es tanto la reproducción de un modelo
> externo cuanto el alma de ese modelo. (*30*, p.21)

Historical reality, then, is for Miró both a point of departure and a
point of return. The artistic transformation of the raw material
drawn from reality and from personal experience takes us back to
reality, but at a much deeper level, at a level, that is, where mean-
ings can be universalized, because Miró is ultimately speaking of
mankind's capacity to inflict unhappiness upon itself by its prone-
ness to a fanatical adherence to particular sets of beliefs.

Since Miró's purpose is to create a fictional world that evokes
a particular aspect of reality, he is discreet in the use of techniques
closely associated with the popular types of fiction, in particular the
complicated, suspense-laden plots of much nineteenth-century
fiction, so much so that his status as novelist was even questioned in
his lifetime. In the Oleza novels character-creation has primacy over
plot, which is not to say that there is no plot, merely that the plot is
of a loose kind rather than a tightly-knit story leading inexorably
towards a pre-planned dénouement. The plot here is the life of
Oleza and the lives of its characters. But within this loose framework there is a perfectly identifiable structure and a clear pattern of
development. We shall look at each volume separately before
studying the links between the two.

Nuestro Padre San Daniel

The novel is divided into four parts, each one longer than the preceding one: Part I, 12 pages; Part II, 44 pages; Part III, 68 pages; Part IV, 90 pages. As one would expect, there is proportionately less description and more action in each successive part, although in broad terms description predominates over action, there being no sustained action but rather a series of events. The main events are five in number: (i) arrival of a new bishop; (ii) arrival of the Carlist agent, Don Alvaro; (iii) engagement and wedding of Don Alvaro and Paulina; (iv) illness and death of Don Daniel; (v) flood and disturbance on the eve of San Daniel leading to the shooting of Don Magín and drowning of Cara-rajada. The rest of the novel is made up of description, dialogue, anecdotes, and minor happenings, all of which have a two-fold function: to portray characters, to evoke atmosphere. Because the novel is not action-oriented, the plot is reduced to a minimum and its development is slow. Just occasionally there are sudden and unexpected incidents (e.g. the appearance of Cara-rajada in front of Paulina or the shooting of Don Magín), but the treatment of these incidents is undramatic. The only incident which could be called melodramatic is that in which Don Alvaro is followed in the dark through the woods by, we are led to believe, a homicidal Cara-rajada, but it turns out to be Elvira, so the incident ends in anticlimax. If we look upon Don Daniel and Paulina as the central characters, that is to say as the characters around whom the novel revolves, we can observe a gradual progression in terms of what happens to the family. The main change in the lives of father and daughter is brought about by the arrival of Don Alvaro and his subsequent marriage to Paulina. The earlier incident in which Cara-rajada frightens Paulina has no immediate repercussions: it serves rather to pre-empt the surprise news that her father is bringing her and to show that Oleza — or the influential Carlists — has made its choice of a husband for Paulina. From the point of view of the Egeas, the main events are the betrothal, the inspection of the new house, the wedding, the separation of father and daughter, Don Daniel's isolation, illness, and death, and Paulina's pregnancy and giving birth to a son. These events all occur towards the end of Part III and in Part IV. On the face of it, therefore, there does seem to be an increasing pace to the novel, but this is more apparent than real, especially as Don Daniel and Paulina by no means dominate the action. They are merely one element of many, though perhaps the single most important one. The headings given to each separate part suggest a much broader interest: I, 'Santas Imágenes'; II, 'Seglares, Capellanes y Prelados'; III, 'Oleza y el Enviado'; IV, 'Oleza y San Daniel'. In addition to these headings, the large number of characters, not all having a connection with the Egeas, suggests that Miró's real subject was not so much the Egea family as the city of Oleza itself.

If we regard Oleza as the real protagonist of the novel, then Miró's development of his material becomes clear. What he has done is gradually to enlarge the picture of life in Oleza, by adding more and more characters, by describing characters' behaviour in particular situations, and by including a few, but only a few, fleeting moments of more rapid action to mask, or compensate for, the very slow pace of the plot.

Part I sets the scene by tracing the ecclesiastical history of Oleza. Because of its history, the city is intimately and irremediably tied to religion, a religion based on dubious miracles and superstition, to say nothing of the strange competitive worship of their respective saints between those who engage in the cult of San Daniel and those who favour the cult of Nuestra Señora. The entire town seems to revolve around the cult of the two images, and the cult affects the names of its streets and even its enterprises. The first part is an indication of what is to follow: a town whose life is totally dominated by religion and which finds itself overwhelmingly under the influence of the clergy.

Part II introduces several of the major characters: Don Daniel Egea, Padre Bellod, Don Amancio Espuch, Doña Corazón, Don Jeromillo, Don Magín, and other ones in passing, such as Don Cruz, Don Vicente Grifol, and the Egeas' maidservant Jimena. Amidst the general description of the characters Miró intersperses a few anecdotes and incidents which largely serve in any case to illuminate facets of character: the death of the old bishop, the confrontation between Doña Corazón's husband and Don Vicente Grifol, and finally, in present novelistic time, the arrival of the new bishop, who appears to be very different from the old.

The arrival of the Bishop at the end of Part II is followed by the arrival of Don Alvaro at the beginning of Part III. These two arrivals are going to represent two rather different approaches to religion and to evoke rather different responses among the *olecenses*. In effect they represent the external forces used by the novelist to break the status quo; that is to say, they are forces for change within the plot-structure of the novel, though not necessarily within Oleza. But Part III, despite its title, is by no means wholly devoted to 'el enviado', the Carlist agent Don Alvaro. Miró continues to expand the range of characters with the homeopath Monera, the epileptic Cara-rajada, Elvira Galindo, and a few other more minor ones. Don Alvaro is present in person in just three of the seven chapters. Quantitatively Cara-rajada's role is just as important: first we hear something of his plight from his mother, and then he is introduced in person in one of the few dramatic incidents in the novel. Miró then proceeds to enlarge upon his depiction of Oleza by following Don Magín through the poor quarter of the city, while using this very excursion to tell us more of Cara-rajada. The connection between these two characters is further developed when Cara-rajada confides in Don Magín, but the subject of their exchange is Don Alvaro, and in this way Miró is able to maintain some degree of unity in what is rapidly turning out to be a gallery of characters. For a time it looks very much as if what we are getting here is the conventional complication of a novelesque intrigue typical of the nineteenth-century *novela de folletín*, but the appearance is deceptive. This apparent complication in the plot, with the antagonism between Cara-rajada and Don Alvaro, will soon run out of steam without having advanced it in any major way. On the other hand we have learnt a good deal about the personalities of Cara-rajada and Don Alvaro.

Part IV stretches from the wedding of Don Alvaro and Paulina to the birth of Pablo some nine to ten months later, but covers many other aspects besides. Again character and atmosphere quite clearly predominate over plot and even, one could say, over incident. There are incidents, of course, but they are neither numerous nor of lasting impact in changing the gradual unfolding of the storyline, the major one being the disturbances which occur on the eve of the patron saint of Oleza. New characters continue to appear: Mossen Orduña, the archivist, and, more briefly, the Count and Countess of Lóriz. Existing characters are further developed. The emphasis, even at this late stage in the novel, is on broadening the picture rather than on closure or radical innovation. In a scene in the episcopal palace we witness the friendship that has developed between Don Magín and the Bishop, a particularly important development from the point of view of the work as a whole. We observe Doña Corazón's fruitless attempt to talk to Paulina and her defeat at the hands of Elvira, now turned into Paulina's severest guardian. We watch Don Alvaro's attempt to get a grip on himself and overcome his fear and loathing of Cara-rajada, who has taken to stalking him. We see Don Daniel's illness and death, and Don Alvaro's and Elvira's determination to keep the pregnant Paulina from venturing out in public to visit her father. We witness the shooting of Don Magín in the middle of a public riot and the drowning of Cara-rajada in the swollen river, both events occurring almost simultaneously in the only chapter to contain incidents of a dramatic nature. Immediately after these incidents the novel reverts to its slow tempo with static scene followed by static scene; but it is these static scenes that tell us most about the nature of Oleza society. Don Jeromillo becomes for a brief time the centre of attention as he takes the wounded Don Magín into his house and visitors congregate in his rooms. The volume ends where it begins, in church, a highly symbolic ending as we see Paulina frantic to get out, terrified by the feeling that she is being buried alive in the church of Nuestro Padre San Daniel.

El obispo leproso

The biggest difference between the two volumes is in the time-span of each. Whereas Volume I spans a period of a year and a half (from the beginning of April in Year 1 to the end of October in Year 2), Volume II covers a much longer period, about nine or ten years (internal inconsistencies impede greater precision). But this difference in time-span is deceptive. At a certain point in Volume II there is a very rapid passage of time; in other words not all nine or ten years are novelized. Pablo goes from being an eight-year-old in Part I (his first year at school) to being a fifteen- or sixteen-year-old in Part II (where he is already in his last year at school). The intervening seven or eight years are barely dealt with at all, so that the bulk of the novel from Part II until the closing chapter covers, in present novelistic time, the deceptively short span of little more than a year, indeed rather less than a year up to the death of the Bishop.

Volume II is considerably longer than Volume I: a third as long again. It is divided into seven parts ranging in length from 22 to 57 pages, with the longer parts being towards the centre. The structure is also more complex than that of the preceding volume, partly because the chronology is more complicated, with excursions from present novelistic time to past novelistic time, and partly because there are more narrative strands, though these are so skilfully interwoven that the reader barely notices the shift from one to the other. The storyline has three major strands: Pablo's childhood and adolescence; María Fulgencia's adolescence and marriage; the Bishop's illness and death. In addition there are subsidiary strands which complicate the storyline without changing it fundamentally: the relationship Alvaro-Paulina-Máximo; the Jesuits and their relations with the Bishop, the Galindos and the Lórizs; the machinations and final disgrace of Elvira; the Don Magín-Purita relationship. In *El obispo leproso* Miró eschews the descriptive and historical preamble of *Nuestro Padre San Daniel*. Part I opens with Pablo escaping from his dreary home to join Don Magín and the Bishop, proceeds with the determination of his father, on the advice of his Carlist friends, to intern Pablo in 'Jesús', follows this with a description of the Jesuit school, and ends with the introduction of the leprosy theme as Don Vicente Grifol examines the Bishop.

Part II brings María Fulgencia into the picture up to the point where, at age seventeen, she joins the convent of La Visitación, not before seeing Pablo Galindo in the street. Part III, which goes back in time, is more wide-ranging and covers various aspects of life in

Oleza by the expedient of reintroducing several of the characters from Volume I (Doña Corazón, Doña Purita) and by having Don Magín informing the Count and Countess (and thereby the reader) of the events that have taken place since their departure from Oleza eight years before.

Part IV is equally diverse, although the emphasis falls heavily on religious activity, both in and out of the cloisters. María Fulgencia's story advances with the reappearance of Mauricio, and Paulina's with the reappearance in her life of her youthful love, Máximo the painter. The Bishop meanwhile has become seriously ill and his condition is public knowledge. Pablo's adolescent sensitivities become apparent when he finds himself among the young women of the Lóriz household for the Holy Week processions. Part V, continuing the religious theme, revolves around the festivity of Corpus Christi, with the Jesuits becoming the focus of attention. The Galindo household shows increasing signs of stress: Elvira's jealousy of her sister-in-law reaches pathological proportions as she prevents her from attending prizegiving and takes Paulina's place alongside her brother; Pablo resents his mother's absence and rebels against his father and aunt.

Part VI takes us back to María Fulgencia, but with Pablo now out of school, Miró is ready to develop the love complication he had been planning all along since the introduction of the new character in Part II. María Fulgencia's marriage to Don Amancio is too precipitate to be credible but it makes possible the much more credible relationship between the two young people. Two of the three major strands of the story thus coalesce. The third, that of the Bishop, hovering in the background, is also brought in via Pablo's visit to the episcopal palace in a bid to save the family estate of El Olivar, and the connection is reinforced in Part VII. In this final part the Bishop gives his blessing to Pablo as he is on his way to the last encounter with María Fulgencia. As a result of the illicit relationship the latter is forced to leave Oleza, as is Elvira Galindo, while the defeated Don Alvaro retires with his family to El Olivar. But the innocent, too, suffer a kind of defeat as Miró winds his story down. The Bishop's departure is more final, Purita's more poignant, and only Don Magín is left in place, a symbol of solitude in the new Oleza of railways and commercial enterprise with the concomitant loss of interest in matters religious.

As in *Nuestro Padre San Daniel*, in *El obispo leproso* Miró does not concentrate the action on a few main characters but disperses it over a fairly large number, both major and minor, each contributing to the wider picture of Oleza society. A tangential but nevertheless major figure in Volume I was Cara-rajada. His place is occupied in Volume II by María Fulgencia. Neither of them would appear to be an essential or representative part of the society of Oleza that Miró is depicting; yet both have an important effect on other characters. Miró's efforts in the area of characterization are sustained, even intensified in Volume II. Miró has felt it necessary to introduce quite a number of new personages. In addition to María Fulgencia (almost certainly created before the publication of *Nuestro Padre San Daniel*, to judge from Miró's references; *31*, pp.17–18), there are several new characters with minor roles: Señor Hugo, the gymnastics teacher; Don Roger, the music teacher; Mauricio, María Fulgencia's cousin; Diego the hunchback, Don Amancio's nasty nephew (given a passing mention in Volume I); Doña Nieves (again merely mentioned in Volume I), who replaces La Amortajadora; Monseñor Salom, the visitor from Aleppo; and then a whole troop of nuns of La Salesa (Madre Clavaria, Madre Abadesa) and of Jesuits from 'Jesús' (Padre Rector, Padre Prefecto, etc.). Several of the major characters from Volume I are further developed in Volume II. This is especially true of Elvira, Paulina, and Don Magín. Some of the minor characters from Volume I are given expanded roles, to the point where they become virtually major characters in Volume II (Purita, the Dean), or at any rate more prominent than in Volume I (Las Catalanas, Lóriz and wife, Máximo, brother of the Countess). Pablo, of course, is a special case, for although he is the closest Miró comes to creating a protagonist, he belongs almost exclusively to Volume II.

Despite the five-year gap in their publication, Miró obviously regarded the two volumes as a single, unified work, and seems to have expected the reader of Volume II to have read Volume I. There are many references in *El obispo leproso* to *Nuestro Padre San Daniel*, references which have both a structural and a reinforcing function: they establish links with the earlier volume and they remind the reader of the importance of what has been said before.

At the beginning of the story of María Fulgencia we read that for her uncle, the Dean, 'las cosas y los hombres eran según eran' (II, p.121), a philosophy repeated a few pages later (II, p.127). The phrase is in reported speech, an echo of the original phrase in direct speech in Volume I: 'Las cosas son según son' (I, p.82), and it is this reported speech that gives the allusions their referential quality. They look back to what the Dean had actually said, indicating the existence of a precedent. There is moreover a structural reflection: for just as in Volume I there had been two references to the Dean's philosophy of life (I, pp.82 and 99), now in Volume II there are also two allusions (II, pp.121 and 127), exactly paralleling the earlier use of the Dean's axiom.

There are many references in *El obispo leproso* to events in *Nuestro Padre San Daniel* where familiarity with this volume is virtually essential for a full understanding: 'Esta doña Purita, tan hermosa, que ustedes ya conocen desde mi herida de San Daniel', says Don Magín (II, p.151) referring to Purita's appearance during his periood of convalescence in Don Jeromillo's house (I, pp.261–66). And he also announces to the Lórizs, who have been living away from Oleza for eight years, the death of Cara-rajada's mother and of Mossen Orduña, characters from Volume I who do not appear in Volume II. Miró is evidently at pains to let the reader know why certain characters do not reappear, but this reader of *El obispo leproso* that Miró has in mind would need to have read *Nuestro Padre San Daniel*. On another occasion, the narrator, reflecting Don Alvaro's thoughts, says: '¡Echar a esa hermana de supremas virtudes, la que se olvidó hasta de su recato de mujer, siguiéndole una noche, con disfraz de hombre, por guardarle de los peligros de Cara-rajada!' (II, p.98). Again, this allusion in Volume II to an episode in Volume I will be devoid of meaning to someone who has not read the earlier volume. A final example occurs towards the end of Volume II and refers back to a scene that took place halfway through Volume I as Paulina now recalls the Bishop's arrival in El Olivar at the time when Don Alvaro was requesting her hand in marriage, an allusion that bridges a gap of some seventeen years of novelistic time. Clearly Miró, when writing or re-writing *El obispo leproso,* had in mind a readership familiar with *Nuestro Padre San Daniel* and wished to remind them of the events in the earlier volume. Occasionally Miró's tactic is overdone and probably fails to achieve its intended effect. When Jimena says, '¡Por algo mientras casaban a Paulina le pedí yo a Dios que me diera coraje y maldad para defenderla de todos!' (II, p.182), it is highly unlikely that the reader would recall Jimena's words in Volume I: 'Mientras te casaban estuve pidiéndole a Dios y al Santo que si no te hacen feliz que me den coraje y maldad para defenderte de todos' (I, p.190). Although we could credit the maidservant herself with a remarkable feat of memory, few readers would be able to emulate her. Nevertheless, even if the reader fails to make the connection, Miró's intention of establishing continuity between the volumes is not to be doubted.

2. Style and Narrative Technique

Miró's richness of style, his sculptured expression, his wealth of vocabulary, his evocative descriptions, led to his being considered not so much a novelist as a poet writing in prose. In a pioneering essay on *Nuestro Padre San Daniel*, L.J. Woodward showed how grievously this view underestimated the substance of Miró's novel, for the brilliant imagery employed by the novelist had a symbolic function that underscored the meaning of the work: 'Il est clair que Miró emploie ses images non comme simple moyen de stylistique, mais comme fonction nécessaire de son oeuvre' (*32*, p.123). The use of images to evoke mood, reflect mental state, or suggest a character's outlook is one of the fundamentals of Miró's style in the Oleza novels. Very often these images are based on natural phenomena, particularly light and shade. Whenever Don Alvaro or his close associates like his sister or Padre Bellod are present or invoked, nature appears sombre, the natural light of the sun is attenuated or replaced by that of oil-lamps; yet when it is Don Magín who is present the sun seems to project its life-giving light and warmth all around.[3] In addition to images based on light and its many variations there are images based on water, on flowers, on fruit. As Pablo sets off for what will be his first meeting with María Fulgencia, Miró describes the scene: 'Olor de nardos recién abiertos; la ribera transparentaba lejanías con promesas de felicidad; los árboles del río incendiaban el azul con sus follajes de oro. La

---

[3]'Le contraste entre ceux qui acceptent la vie et ceux qui la rejettent [...] est eclairé, établi par tout un réseau d'images basé sur la clarté et les ténèbres', writes L. J. Woodward (*32*, p.122).

misma limpidez y fragancia del aire tenían los pensamientos de Pablo' (II, p.330). His sensual yet comparatively innocent love affair with María Fulgencia in the orchard — the adolescent discovery of love — is thus set in a symbolic Garden of Eden, evoked by the foregoing lines and confirmed later: 'Todo rodeándole para que él lo poseyese. Así contemplaría el primer hombre la creación intacta delante de sus ojos y de sus rodillas' (II, p.354). Particularly interesting in this connection is Miró's use of the lemon as a symbol, not of bitterness, but of purity (26, p.115). Pablo's and María Fulgencia's love affair is conducted under the symbol of the lemon: 'Fue Pablo al comedor y vino con un limón como un fragante ovillo de luz [...]. La fruta juntaba sus manos y sus respiraciones. Recibían y transpiraban el mismo aroma' (II, p.337); and it is under the lemon tree in the orchard that they kiss. When Pablo goes into the palace gardens he sees the Bishop seated in his old favourite spot at the foot of the lemon tree. The fruit reminds Pablo of María Fulgencia, a pure and virginal María Fulgencia, with her 'candidez de virgen y de flor de limón' (II, p.353). The Bishop, the real 'hombre puro' of the novel, confirms this association of the lemon tree with purity: 'Subió el obispo sus manos para perfumárselas en las hojas tiernas del limón; y las vio llagadas y no quiso tocar la hermosura del árbol' (II, p.353).

Frequently Miró evokes atmosphere by a sustained onrush of nouns: instead of painstaking description we get stark enumeration; verbs disappear. The list can be of streets, of flowers, of trees, of fragrances, of sweetmeats, of furniture: 'Y yo tenía repartido el casón: las habitaciones altas para ellos, con muebles de mis abuelos y de mis padres, muebles de árboles de heredades de mi familia, de cipreses, de olivos, de almeces, de sabinas, de nogales, de moreros' (I, p.174). Sometimes the enumeration is a miscellany of sights, sounds and smells meant to evoke the characteristic qualities of the life of Oleza:

> Dulcerías, jardines, incienso, campanas, órgano, silencio, trueno de molinos y de río; mercado de frutas; persianas cerradas; azoteas de cal y sol; vuelos de

palomos; tránsito de seminaristas con sotanilla y beca de
tafetán; de colegiales con uniforme de levita y fajín azul;
de niñas con bandas de grana y cabellos nazarenos;
procesiones; hijas de María; camareras del Santísimo;
Horas Santas; tierra húmeda y caliente; follajes
pomposos; riegos y ruiseñores; nubes de gloria; montes
desnudos. (II, p.94)

Long as the quotation may appear, it is just half of the original
description. Yet prolixity is not a charge one could justifiably level
at Miró. On the contrary: the technique is very effective in capturing
the essence of the city without having to interpose conventional
descriptions which would indeed appear lengthy and intrusive. In
the example just cited we move from the thoughts and conversation
of a group of people talking about their town, to an evocation of the
town itself, and then back to the group in a natural progression, so
that the description appears part of the narrative rather than an
intromission.

Miró's expression can be and often is succinct yet enormously
suggestive. His brilliant phraseology can insinuate a great deal in a
very few words. When he describes the Bishop's sermon as 'sin un
plañido retórico de ternura de *Nos*' (I, p.109), he is insinuating the
Bishop's simplicity as a preacher and as a man, his dislike of protocol, his distance from traditional pomp and convention, his refusal
to play to the gallery, his determination to be his own man rather
than the figure others expect him to be, his directness and compo-
sure, and he is suggesting at the same time that the new Bishop may
be bringing new attitudes along with his new style. When three lines
further on he describes the Jesuit Fathers attending the Bishop's
reception as 'de una palidez de escogida santidad' (I, p.109), he is
not only insinuating much the opposite of the Jesuits — they are
poseurs, playing at being holy, hypocritical — but is hinting at a
possible clash between the two attitudes. It would be otiose to
continue giving examples of this kind of condensed expression
pregnant with meaning; there are hundreds of instances in the
Oleza novels. There is, however, a most interesting comment made

by Miró à propos of *El obispo leproso* which is well worth quoting:
'Creo que en el *El obispo leproso* se afirma más mi concepto sobre
la novela: decir las cosas por insinuación.'[4] It is this idea of narrating where possible through suggestion rather than through direct
statement that lies behind this technique and others used by Miró in
the Oleza novels.

Another essential quality of Miró's style is the use he makes
of ironic or gently mocking touches, often in connection with
character portrayal. The ironic tone tends to be of a humorous rather
than a mordant kind, though it can also at times imply severe
criticism. When, referring to the miracle of the olive tree turned
laurel, he writes that 'es preferible admitir el milagro que escarbar
en sus fundamentos vegetales' (I, p.58), he is poking gentle fun at
the Church's, or the faithful's, tendency to prefer miracles to
common sense, a theme that will reappear later in the novel. Miró's
depiction of the Madres Salesas is never hostile; but this does not
prevent him from passing ironic comment on the Order's absurd
faith in its relic: '[...] temía los peligros y la irreverencia de confiar
la preciosa reliquia al servicio de Correos entre estampas inmundas,
impresos, cartas de herejes y pliegos de valores declarados de la
banca judía difundida por todo el mundo. La comunidad de Nuestra
Señora horrorizóse imaginándolo. Durante algunos días vivieron
consternadas las dulces religiosas' (II, p.190). The mechanical crib
exhibited at Christmas time at Gil Rebollo's is described sardonically and ambiguously as a 'farsa sagrada' (II, p.159), by contrast to
the *autos* and other religious plays put on by the Jesuit school, but
on another level it is farcical too in its mock-realism and in the
excitement it generates because it is the only spectacle in Oleza to
allow a mixed audience. The volumes in the Carlist Club are
perused by Pablo 'como si fuesen lápidas' (II, p.320), that is, a mere
curiosity in a decaying establishment. Don Amancio expresses
himself with 'una elegancia verdaderamente latina' (I, p.81), in
other words he is pompous, verbose and theatrical. At the special
ceremony to mark the end of the school year at 'Jesús', 'los

---

[4]*Obras Completas de Gabriel Miró*, Edición Conmemorativa, I (1932), p.x.

invitados, singularmente las mujeres de más elegancia y belleza, eran tan dichosos que se sobresaltaban de serlo, y no sabiendo qué hacer ni qué pensar, daban gracias a Dios' (II, p.258), which is a more subtle way of saying that their religious fervour is a mechanical substitute for their inability to do or think anything else. And when, with an enviable economy of expression, he describes Elvira as 'grifada de honestidad' (II, p.164) and as having 'bascas de pureza' (II, p.275), the ironic turn of phrase serves his critical purpose infinitely better than any straight 'telling' could have done.[5]

Turning now from style to narrative technique in the narrower sense, several general aspects should be noted, however summarily. The predominance of character-portrayal over action was mentioned in the preceding chapter; individual characters will be studied in the chapters that follow. As far as Miró's technique is concerned it is worth noting here that he often sees characters as complete wholes in which physical and moral attributes are virtually inseparable. Don Magín cuts an imposing figure, head held high, hat worn well back, forehead open to the sun and nostrils ready to catch the many and varied fragrances as he perambulates around the town; his religious attitude is likewise open, tolerant, enlightened and questioning. Father Bellod's main physical characteristic is that he is blind in one eye; and this univision is reflected in his narrow-minded view of life and religion. Elvira is described as having 'un movimiento de sierpe' (I, p.177), and she will turn out to have a viper's tongue too. Don Alvaro is described as having 'manos enjutas de asceta' (I, p.117) and a beard 'más de fray que de galán caballero' (I, p.122), and he will turn out to live his married life more like a monk than a spouse. One needs care, however, in inter-

---

[5]For more on Miró's use of irony and humour see the material collected by Yvette Miller (*19*, pp.123–45 and 165–73), and also the separate essay by the same author, 'La ironía y el humor en la novelística de Gabriel Miró', in *Homenaje a Gabriel Miró: estudios de crítica literaria*, ed. J.L. Román del Cerro (Alicante: Caja de Ahorros Provincial, 1979), pp.161–83. It is worth noting that, serious as Miró's theme undoubtedly is, the novel is rich in humorous scenes.

preting these outward signs. The Bishop's leprosy, for example, is an indication not of moral decay but of pain and suffering endured in isolation.

Allusion is another of Miró's narrative techniques, at times direct and obvious, at times oblique and subtle. A great many of these allusions are biblical, although there are several historical and literary ones too, for example to the fourteenth-century *Libro de Buen Amor*. To the lay reader not familiar with religious writings, the references, both explicit and implicit, to ecclesiastical history and the Bible can be a source of puzzlement (for example, the Bishop's account of leprosy, which is taken from Leviticus in the Old Testament without the source being mentioned), but an annotated edition or bibliographical research will resolve most of the difficulties. There are, however, a number of latent references which can easily pass unnoticed or which leave us uncertain as to whether they really contain allusions. When the Segral bursts its banks in *Nuestro Padre San Daniel*, is there a hidden allusion to the Book of Daniel, 9:26, as G.G. Brown argued, or was it simply suggested to Miró by the periodical overflowing of the river Segura in Orihuela? Is Father Bellod right when he refers to the flooding as 'el diluvio de la ira divina' (I, p.250), or is Don Jeromillo right when he refers to the flooding as unimportant, 'la de menos daño de todas las de Oleza' (I, p.262)? If there is an intended biblical allusion, as appears to be the case here, then it is hard to avoid the conclusion that Miró is in a way subverting the biblical view of flood as divine punishment (just as Don Magín himself had done earlier in the story). The fictional Segral bursts its banks for exactly the same reason that the real Segura does. But Miró makes it happen unseasonably, on the eve of San Daniel, in order to relate it to the religious theme running through the book. The biblical metaphor, however, turns out to be a curiously empty one. Oleza gets its feet wet and is soon back to normal: there is no cataclysm.[6]

---

[6]With reference to this episode and Don Jeromillo's comment, Yvette Miller writes: 'La deflación de la causa tiene un marcado tono irónico' (*19*, p.100).

A similar case is that of the killing of one of María Fulgencia's two turtle doves, in which it is difficult not to see an echo (once G.G. Brown had pointed it out) of Leviticus, 14, where there are several references to a pair of birds one of which is killed in sacrifice. Yet the point of the episode in Miró is entirely different from that of the biblical version. For the reason that one of María Fulgencia's birds is killed is the horrifying thought that they might be of the opposite sex. In other instances the case for biblical allusion is even more circumstantial. The episode in which the Bishop tells his servants not to rebuke young Pablo but to allow him to play and shout, and then awaits the child's appearance and strikes up a friendship with him, is surely an echo of 'Suffer the little children and forbid them not to come unto me' (St Matthew, 19:13–14), an echo the effect of which is to suggest an association Bishop-Christ. But at the same time the Bishop's Christ-like preference for children is Miró's way of establishing a stark contrast with the doctrine propounded by Don Cruz, who says that for parents to enjoy their children is potentially sinful, and with the practice implemented by Don Alvaro, who manifests a total lack of affection for his son. The association Bishop-Christ is in any case explicitly made on another occasion when the narrator reflects Pablo's thoughts: '¿No era la voz [the Bishop's] como la voz del Señor cuando reconviene al que se aparta de su gracia?' (II, p.353). If association is one aspect of Miró's technique, dissociation or contrast is the other side of the coin. There are contrasting characters (Don Magín-Father Bellod, Doña Elvira-Purita), contrasting episodes (the Catalanas' *tertulia* followed by Doña Corazón's *tertulia*, the María Fulgencia-Pablo sexual encounter versus the Elvira-Pablo sexual encounter), contrasting houses (El Olivar-Don Alvaro's), even two contrasting Olezas: 'La vieja Oleza se quedó mirando a la Oleza de los Lóriz' (II, p.213). Contrast is such a fundamental technique and its use so all-pervasive that we shall encounter numerous and varied examples in the chapters that follow.

Another characteristic technique, if rather more sparingly used, is that of repetition. We saw in the previous chapter that Volume II repeats or recalls certain statements from Volume I.

Repetition of tiny details, however, also occurs within the same volume. On being introduced to the Jesuit school we learn that 'como a la misma hora — diez y media — se daban en 'Jesús' las clases de Gimnasia y Música [...], el señor Hugo llegaba al colegio con don Roger' (II, p.109). Many chapters and many years later they are still arriving at school together at precisely the same time: 'Don Roger y el Sr Hugo, que entraban juntos en 'Jesús' todos los días, a las diez y media [...]' (II, p.283). The Recreo Benéfico, which the Jesuits see as the work of the impious freemasons, 'caridad inspirada por las tinieblas de las Logias', holds 'veladas, comedias, tómbolas, cosos, jiras' (II, pp.271–72) in order to undermine the good habits of the population. The idea is repeated later in the novel in almost identical language: 'El Recreo Benéfico, con su mote masónico de caridad, iba pudriendo las limpias costumbres. Muñía bailes, jiras, cosos, tómbolas, comedias y verbenas, que condenaba implacable' (II, p.305). Such repetitions serve a double purpose: they reinforce the unity and continuity of the narrative, and, on the ideological level, they emphasize the theme of tradition versus innovation, of sameness versus change.

The mode of narration of the Oleza novels presents no major problems, although one particular aspect does call for some degree of awareness. As far as narrative voice is concerned, Miró uses impersonal, omniscient, third-person narration virtually throughout, but this needs qualification in a number of ways. There are a few occasions where the narrator uses the first person, both singular and plural, these self-references occurring in a quite specific context. 'He visto un óleo del señor Espuch y Loriga'(I, p.55), he says of the late chronicler of Oleza, and then refers to 'nuestro episcopologio' (I, p.56). A few pages later, referring to the records of the treasures of the church of Nuestro Padre San Daniel, he writes: 'Y no contaré los hacheros, candeleros, vinajeras [...]' (I, p.62). In Volume II in a further reference to the writings of Espuch y Loriga, this time on the foundation of the Jesuit school, he writes: 'Yo he leído casi todo el manuscrito, y he visitado muchas veces los edificios [...]' (II, p.99). What these first-person interventions have in common is the I-as-witness approach to the narrative that is to follow: the narrator is assuring us that he has the necessary knowledge to narrate. He has been to the place where the events have occurred and he has consulted the works of a respected local historian. The device has an ancient pedigree, though Miró, like Cervantes in *Don Quixote*, is using it ironically. When he says he visited the Jesuit school he is of course making an enormous understatement, since Miró was a pupil at the Jesuit school in Orihuela for five years. The appeal to historical authority in the person of Espuch y Loriga is ironic in another way, for not only is Espuch y Loriga fictitious but Miró's scattered references to this character make it plain that he is satirizing a particular type of amateur local historian full of self-importance, given to writing in inflated style and to making emphatic assertions. Yet, despite the satire, the narrator's admission of his use of others' writings is a direct reflection of Miró's own use of real documents.

The one aspect of Miró's narrative style that can lead the inattentive reader astray is his use of *style indirect libre*, or indirect free speech, in which a narrator reports the thoughts or comments of a character without a specific indication to that effect. It is easy, but potentially erroneous, to ascribe to the narrator, or even worse the author, views that belong solely to the character. A number of examples will help to elucidate Miró's use of this technique.

When, in the context of the rainstorm on the eve of San Daniel, we read the following sentence: 'Ni ferias, ni milagros, ni regocijos, por culpa de unas obras malintencionadas' (I, p.251), it is important to realize that the feelings of frustration that are being conveyed are not the narrator's but those of the members of the Carlist Club. The provenance of the accusation contained in the label 'malintencionadas' will be apparent provided we remember that it was Father Bellod and his companions who had objected to the restoration work in the church of San Daniel in the first place.

Following a description of Oleza in summer, we read:

Siempre lo mismo; pero quizá los tiempos fermentasen
de peligros de modernidad. Palacio mostraba una indife-
rencia moderna. Don Magín paseaba por el pueblo como
un capellán castrense. Y esos Lóriz, de origen liberal, y

> otros por el estilo, se aficionaban al ambiente viejo y
> devoto como a una golosía de sus sentidos, imaginando
> suyo lo que sólo era de Oleza: sus piadosas delicias, su
> sangre tan especiada, sus esencias de tradición, el fervor
> y el olor vegetal, arcaico y litúrgico, se convertían para
> los tibios en elementos y convites de pecado. (II, p.95)

It is all too easy to take a passage such as this at face value and
forget that the description had commenced two pages earlier with a
reference to Don Amancio: '[...] la ciudad se quedaba lo mismo. Lo
reconocía Don Amancio' (II, p.93). In other words, the comment
about the Bishop, Don Magín, the Lórizs and the *tibios* is not an
objective part of the narration but has been refracted through the
mind of Don Amancio and thereby acquired very particular
overtones. A similar example occurs during a *tertulia* at the house
of Las Catalanas:

> Ella [Elvira] bien sabía que en todos los tiempos hubo
> males y escándalos en Oleza. Lo sabía por Don
> Amancio. ¡Qué saber de hombre! Desde que se dejaba la
> barba parecía más mozo: una barba lisa hasta el pecho,
> una barba preciosa de color de azafrán ... Pero en otros
> tiempos no contaba Oleza con partidos como el que
> representaba su hermano don Alvaro, y más atras, ni
> siquiera hubo obispo en Oleza. Ahora, en cambio,
> parecía no haberlo. Porque con un obispo enfermo, y un
> enfermo como ése, iba pudriéndose la diócesis. (II,
> p.169)

The intercalated reference to Don Amancio and ensuing suspension
points might induce the reader to accept what follows as information coming directly from the narrator. In fact we are still receiving
the comments of Elvira, who is blaming the Bishop for the moral
decay of Oleza. In this instance Miró chooses to dispel any possible
doubt by returning to Elvira at the start of the next paragraph: 'Aquí
Elvira les avisó [...]'.

There are instances in which the use of *style indirect libre* is particularly subtle. At the leave-taking after the prize-giving ceremony in 'Jesús' we are given a description of the guests filing out: 'Iba delante Máximo con doña Purita. Parecía increíble que esta mujer no se sintiese rechazada por todos los corazones de "Jesús"' (II, p.274). Whose thought is this? Hardly Máximo's, since he has no reason to think of Purita in those terms. Is the narrator speaking to us directly? The next sentence might appear to suggest this since it contains factual information: 'Era la primera en asistir a las fiestas y comedias benéficas, y en un reciente ensayo no bajó de las tablas por la gradilla, sino de los brazos del galán y le soltó su risa en medio de la boca como si lo rociase de besos.' Yet given what we, and the narrator, know of Purita's character, the sentiment expressed in the second sentence quoted above — feeling rejected and opting out of life — is not one we would expect the narrator to ascribe to her. It is the sentence that follows that provides the clue: 'Se sabía en "Jesús".' The factual information has been processed at the Jesuit establishment. And the final sentence of the paragraph confirms that the view of Purita which we are getting is that of the Padre Rector: 'Y el rector dolióse con los condes de la perniciosa generosidad en las amistades, y Purita le atendía, brillándole en la mirada una lucecita de insolencia' (II, p.274).

Some passages in which *style indirect libre* occurs are particularly complex because direct personal comment from the narrator also occurs:

> Acabado el oficio y rezo, y después del refectorio, juntóse la comunidad en la sala de costura. No quiso la prelada el coro ni la sala de Capítulo ni otro lugar de ceremonia, temerosa de los efectos extáticos. *¡Señor, arrobos no! Un aposento apacible y claro, donde se habla con sencillez y honestísimos júbilos, no había de invitar a demasiados prodigios.* <u>Por humilde olvidaba la madre que el recinto del milagro es la simplicidad de los corazones. Llamado San Goar por su obispo, acude a Palacio; pasa a la antecámara; no ve percha ni mueble</u>

<u>donde dejar su capa, y la cuelga de un rayo de sol. De
una devanadera podía temer la madre que se quedaran
prendidos como flores los anhelos de sor María
Fulgencia.</u> La miraron todas, y ella se puso colorada, y
estaba más hermosa (II, p.191).

Here we have a mixture of ordinary objective narration, *style
indirect libre*, and personal comment, which for the sake of clarity
have been indicated in the passage in roman type, italic type and
underlined type. The last phrase, however, is a problem: who
observes the enhanced beauty of María Fulgencia? The nuns, in
which case it is *style indirect libre*, or the narrator, in which case it
is a personal comment?

The use of *style indirect libre* avoids the tedious repetition
associated with conventional reported speech: it takes us inside the
consciousness of a character without the obvious intrusion of the
narrator. But notwithstanding Miró's frequent use of this technique
the narrator's presence is far from invisible. There are numerous
occasions on which the direct and personal intervention of a
narrating mind occurs, that is to say, where the narrator interposes
his own views. Thus, when, in the context of Don Alvaro's
defensive reaction to the Bishop's expressed surprise at finding him
still in Oleza, we read: 'Para una virtud tenebrosa, nada tan acerbo
como una sospecha de ruindad' (I, p.170), it is clear that this
generalization is not the character's but the narrator's and that it
contains the latter's moral judgment of the character. Or again,
when in the description of the Hermano Inspector's outraged
reaction to Perceval's semi-sexual interest in the statue of the
Roman goddess, we come across the parenthetical remark '(un
Santo Padre ha dicho que el hábito de la castidad endurece las
entrañas)' (II, p.216), we know that the narrator is signalling his
disapproval of the harsh puritanism of the Jesuit.

One final but important aspect of Miró's technique remains to
be studied: the temporal framework he has chosen to give his novel
and the indirect way in which he establishes this framework by
reference to events, time of year and elapsed time. In this context

references to historical events are not particularly significant: Miró uses these in a loose manner to evoke a particular historical age rather than to establish a precise chronology. In Volume I, for example, there are references to the Pretender Carlos VII's voyages overseas (1884–85) and to the execution of Francisco Otero after his attempted assassination of King Alfonso XII (1880), but in the novel they appear in the wrong chronological order. More significant from the point of view of Miró's technique are the internal references to the calendar. There are regular references to time of year which allow us to insert the events in time with a good deal of accuracy and to establish the correct chronology. Sometimes Miró mentions a month or sometimes a particular feast. For example we are told that Paulina marries on the feast of St John of the Cross, November 24, that four and a half months later she is pregnant, that her father dies in June, and that the baby is expected in September. We are not told the date of Pablo's birth, but Miró evidently had the month of September very much in mind, for other references in Volume II follow on from this: for example, some four weeks before the start of the school year Paulina's objection to Pablo's internment in 'Jesús' is made on the grounds that he is not yet eight. We know therefore that when Pablo starts school on September 15 he must be almost exactly eight years old. The time-scheme in *El obispo leproso* is a good deal more complex and involves Miró in numerous oblique references to time, either with the object of orienting the reader or more likely (since few readers would go to the trouble of reconstructing the internal calendar) of orienting himself. The problem arises for Miró because of the nature of the Bishop's disease. Leprosy is a protracted disease, with periods of remission and regression over a span of many years. Miró has somehow to reconcile this circumstance with the adolescent awakening of Pablo and María Fulgencia. Thus, in the case of Pablo, we move quickly from his first year at school to his last with no reference to the period in between, while in the case of María Fulgencia we are given the necessary antecedents and soon arrive at the point where she is seventeen and, shortly after recovering from typhus, enters the convent of La Visitación, contemporaneous with Pablo being in his final year at school. No such rapid progression is possible in dealing with the course of the Bishop's illness, and the references to it have to be spread out over a time-scale quite different from that of the Pablo-María Fulgencia storyline. Miró's technique consists in slowing down the tempo of the narrative and casually working in references to the Bishop in a series of movements back and forth in time. After he is examined by Don Vicente Grifol the Bishop's health improves, and Miró creates an impression of passing time by his use of the past continuous and imperfect tenses followed by the past historic: 'Se le fueron secando y descamando las cortezas. Ya no le quedaban sino unos rodales morenos sin rebordes, sin deformidad cutánea. Salió en coche. Hizo una visita pastoral y un viaje a Madrid' (II, p.118). This trip to Madrid may well be the same 'viaje a Madrid de Su Ilustrísima' (II, p.149) mentioned later by the Countess to Don Magín, but if so, comparatively little time has elapsed. Two earlier references to the worsening state of the Bishop's health (II, pp.141 and 142), at the time of María Fulgencia's arrival at La Visitación, belong of course to a very much later time. During the early stages of construction of the railway the Bishop is in comparatively good health, but we are not told how long this state of affairs lasts, although the use of the imperfect tense is meant to suggest the passage of time: 'El señor obispo mostraba una infantil complacencia en su salud. Bajaba a su huerto [...]. Los curiales le veían conversar con el hortelano [...]. Daba de comer a los palomos; se sentaba y leía [...]' (II, p.160). The decline in the Bishop's health is also a gradual process and is accompanied by a waning of his public appearances: 'Poco a poco, Su Ilustrísima volvió a sus soledades' (II, p.162). Yet this, bafflingly, is happening at the time of Don Magín's visit to the Lóriz household less than a year after Don Vicente Grifol's death. It is entirely as if the impression of the passage of the years created by Miró's technique were a complete mirage and we had hardly moved forward in time at all. Another example will serve to show both the nature of and the inherent contradiction in Miró's technique. '¡Para qué querrá Su Ilustrísima el tren teniendo que pasar los años escondido arrancándose postemas!' (II, p.171), says the malevolent

Elvira. The phrase 'pasar los años' is naturally meant to convey the slow course of the Bishop's illness, but Elvira's exclamation is made not so long after the return of the Lórizs and arrival of the railway workers, so that to speak of years at this point (when the Bishop's worsening condition has only recently been confirmed) is anachronistic. This is corroborated in the strictly synchronous chapter that follows, in which Don Magín declares that it is exactly a year since the death of Don Vicente Grifol. The impression created by Miró, however, is that of a much longer passage of time. After this point we are firmly in the final year in the Bishop's life and Miró's problem is left behind. His technique in reconciling two asynchronous storylines is only partly successful. It is successful in so far as it gives the reader the necessary impression of elapsed time. It is not successful in so far as it creates chronological inconsistencies.[7]

One other such inconsistency should be mentioned. Despite Miró's obvious interest in establishing an internal calendar for the novel to keep track of elapsed time, he has somehow managed to lose track of one complete year. The inconsistency arises between mother and son. Just before prizegiving at the end of Pablo's schooling Paulina says that Pablo will soon be sixteen, confirming her thoughts two months earlier when, upon meeting her youthful love, Máximo the painter, she says to herself: 'Ya llevaríamos diecisiete años casados desde entonces' (II, p.208). Assuming that she is thinking of that hypothetical marriage as having taken place earlier in the same year as her real marriage (i.e. before the appearance of Don Alvaro), this must mean that her real marriage is sixteen-and-a-half years old (seventeen years old the following November) and that Pablo will be sixteen in September. Paulina's two statements are perfectly consistent. But when Pablo meets María Fulgencia in October he says he is seventeen. When a little later he visits the Bishop's palace and recognizes the cracked paving slab that hides the ants' nest he had watched as a child, he

---

[7]For more on the techniques used by Miró to slow down the tempo and lengthen the time-scale, see Marian Coope (*6*, pp.150–54).

thinks of the nine years that have passed since he last visited the gardens in the company of Don Magín. Since that visit took place immediately before his internment in 'Jesús' at the age of eight, Pablo's reminiscence suggests that he is seventeen. The coincidence of Paulina's contemplation of a missed opportunity — seventeen years of marriage to a much more attractive husband — with Pablo's reference to his age could conceivably suggest a hidden symbolism: Pablo ought to have been the child of a loving relationship instead of that of a loveless one, especially since Máximo shows affection for the boy. The circumstances of Pablo's birth — some ten months after Paulina's marriage to Don Alvaro — are sufficiently clear to preclude any more sinister interpretation. The discrepancy in Pablo's age is probably not of any great importance, but it does serve to indicate Miró's difficulty in ensuring a perfect fit for all the pieces of the chronological jigsaw.

3. Major Characters (1)

The astonishing incomprehension which the Oleza novels met upon their publication is typified by Ortega's allegation that Miró's characters are poorly drawn, mere *figurones* lacking individuality (*25*, p.546). I would argue that, on the contrary, the creation of characters is Miró's greatest achievement in the Oleza novels. The richness of character-portrayal that we find in this work, its depth, variety, and subtlety, is exceptional in the twentieth-century novel, largely preoccupied with philosophical and formal matters, often to the detriment of character-creation. There are fifteen personages that can be considered either central or at any rate major because of their repeated presence in the narrative. They can be divided into three broad categories: five clerics (the Bishop, Father Bellod, Don Cruz, Don Magín and Don Jeromillo); four laymen (Don Daniel, Don Alvaro, Don Amancio and Cara-rajada); and five women (Paulina, Doña Corazón, Doña Elvira, Doña Purita and María Fulgencia). And of course there is Pablo, who comes close to being the protagonist of *El obispo leproso*. There are in addition numerous other characters whose roles in some cases are only slightly less important than those of the ones already mentioned. In this chapter I shall survey the main lay personages, leaving the clergymen for the next.

Don Daniel Egea and his household form the central narrative nucleus of *Nuestro Padre San Daniel*. Don Daniel is the first character about whom we are given a significant amount of information. El Olivar, the large olive plantation inherited by Don Daniel, contains much more than olive trees, and the owner of the estate represents the landowning aristocracy, even if untitled, of traditional stock and solid virtue. He is a man incapable of a mean action or a hurtful word, but a man who is ill-equipped to cope with life on his own. Since he has lost his wife, almost his sole interest in life is his daughter and a few childish pleasures, such as Doña Corazón's caramel custard. When he is deprived of Paulina's presence his terrible sense of loss leads to his death within months. As a Carlist he belongs to the circle of Don Cruz, Don Amancio and Father Bellod, and he is both incapable of standing up to them and all too easily impressed by Don Alvaro and his stories of the Carlist Pretender. The fact that he does not care for 'alborotos y calenturas de partido' (I, p.116) shows that his devotion to Carlism is not fanatical, nor even political, but simply a sentimental attachment to the past: in Don Alvaro's presence 'se fervorizaba su sangre infantil' (I, p.116). The loyalty and reverence he feels for the Carlist cause and its figure-head is not only naïve but also the root of his undoing. Blinded by Don Alvaro's Carlist credentials, even to the extent of believing and taking delight in the unfounded rumour that he is the bastard son of the Pretender, Don Daniel fails utterly to see that Don Alvaro, because of his age and character, is the wrong suitor for his daughter. In Don Daniel Miró has clearly wished to depict a good man but one who is flawed by his incapacity to rebel against the stifling religious atmosphere that surrounds him, indeed incapable even of perceiving it, so hard does tradition weigh upon him. His display of religious reverence for the beret which he thinks has been worn by Don Carlos would be comic if it were not indicative of his tragic inability to tell worthy human qualities from ideological exhibitionism. Don Daniel seems a left-over from another time, incapable in his essential goodness and mental isolation of recognizing duplicity and meanness of spirit. It is his incapacity to see the darker side of people's motives that leads first to Doña Corazón's unhappy marriage and then to Paulina's. In thought, in word, and in deed Don Daniel is a holy fool. His naïvety and unworldliness mark him out as a victim from the start. '¡Mi santo es uno de los más importantes!', he exclaims with childish enthusiasm (I, p.73); but he certainly does not live up to his patron saint's recorded wisdom.[8]

---

[8]Interestingly enough, however, although a poor judge of character, Don Daniel has a momentary insight into Elvira's real nature: 'Don Daniel la miraba, y mirándola se asustó porque de tan casta le parecía una mala

If Don Daniel is a victim, his chosen son-in-law is a victimizer — of his father-in-law, his wife, and his son. But in another sense Don Alvaro is also a victim, a victim of his own expectations of himself. He is one of the most complex characters in the novel, tormented, unhappy, and finally humiliated and defeated spiritually. As an emissary and close servant of Don Carlos he becomes the centre of attention immediately upon his arrival in Oleza. Taking advantage of Don Daniel's boyish enthusiasm for Carlism, he claims the young and beautiful Paulina as his wife. But for all his moral uprightness he is vulnerable and over-sensitive about his intentions. When the Bishop accidentally interrupts his engagement party and expresses his surprise at seeing Don Alvaro still in Oleza, the latter is silently angry, feeling that he is being accused of acting under false pretences: 'Su Ilustrísima le había rebajado delante de su propia conciencia. Porque el recuerdo de los propósitos de su venida al pueblo le traspasó, acusándole de embaucador de dotes' (I, p.170). The very idea of seeing himself as a con-man interested only in the woman's dowry completely unsettles him, such is his opinion of himself. It is for this reason, to live up to his own distorted ideas of uprightness and to prevent others from accusing him of sponging on Don Daniel, that he insists on going to live in an old, gloomy house instead of on the family farm. Not only does he deprive the old man of his happiness, he virtually imprisons Paulina to satisfy his own view of himself as a man of dignity, sobriety, and discipline. He even insinuates to Paulina that he would not welcome the traditional bridal dress at their wedding because he considers it over-glamorous, thus obliging her to give up the bridal gown which she had been looking forward to wearing. His preventing her from going to visit her father on his deathbed or from attending her son's school graduation ceremony, or the extreme authoritarianism to which he subjects Pablo, all verge on cruelty. The only member of

---

mujer; de tan casta, de pensar constantemente en el pecado para aborrecerlo, semejaba que se le quedaran sus señales' (I, p.187). In this way Miró draws a subtle distinction between Don Daniel's conception of virtue and that of Elvira, Alvaro, Don Cruz, and Padre Bellod.

his family to whom he shows any consideration is his sister, but her public self-betrayal leads him to disown her and to retreat in shame. For Don Alvaro virtue is very much a public affair. His virtue and self-sacrifice must be publicly perceived: when everyone else leaves Oleza to avoid the summer heat he makes a point of staying, ignoring the pleas of Paulina and Pablo; he mortgages Paulina's estate to make a donation to the Carlist cause and to *Alba Longa*'s newspaper; and he feels frustration when events rob him of the opportunity to give it away altogether to the Jesuit Fathers. Unlike Pablo, Don Alvaro feels it is important to 'tener razón' (I, p.328), 'ese "tener razón" que desperdiciaba su hijo' (I, p.330). When things go drastically wrong, with the public disgrace of his son, he feels compelled to withdraw from Oleza society and bury himself in the country estate he had for so long spurned.

The trait of Don Alvaro which Miró most emphasizes is his austere and joyless view of life and of religion. The arrival of Don Carlos in Spain, Don Alvaro believes, is not solely dependent on the victory of the army; it is dependent, too, on the moral rearmament of the country; for Spaniards in general and Olezans in particular have forgotten their traditional virtues and surrendered to sensual pleasures. His aversion to any pleasurable experience renders him incapable of human warmth or of any expression of joy; he cannot even allow his wife to sit at the same alms table in church as Purita, for Purita is tainted with the mark of sensuality. Miró's depiction of Don Alvaro as a psychoneurotic with an obsessive fear of sensual gratification of any kind is sustained to the very end. Even in his final retreat at El Olivar he is condemned to restless perambulations like the Wandering Jew, in case a moment of repose might induce a sense of pleasure at the natural surroundings. His austerity and self-negation are fearsome: 'Sería capaz del mal y del bien, de todo menos de entregarse a la exaltación y a la postración de la dulzura de sentirse. No se rompía su dureza de piedra, su inflexibilidad mineralizada en su sangre. Siempre con el horror del pecado' (II, p.370). And yet, for all his asceticism and self-righteousness, Don Alvaro is not at ease with his conscience. He cannot bear the accusing look of Cara-rajada, or the thought that the other despises

him because on that fateful occasion in the past he stood passively
and watched while an innocent man was cruelly murdered on his
wedding day in front of his bride. This act of cowardice haunts Don
Alvaro, and he tries to fight it by going out alone at night where he
knows Cara-rajada might be lurking and thus trying to negate his
fear; but he is careful to take a gun with him. Don Alvaro is an
embittered man; but embittered by his own joyless character rather
than by any extrinsic cause. He imagines his pretty wife married to a
younger, handsome and passionate man, a man with whom Paulina
might enjoy all kinds of sensual and carnal delights that he himself
cannot provide. He hates the thought; he determines to be doubly
austere. But it is his own inability to enjoy the beautiful body of his
wife that makes him insanely and irrationally jealous, jealous
enough to destroy a painting of a martyred virgin with bare breasts
that another man had presented to Paulina. It is his own inadequacy
and emotional frustration that make him abhor all the pleasures of
the senses and adopt harsh and rigorous ways that end in cruelty
towards those that are closest to him. It is the unconventional Don
Magín, echoing Cara-rajada's reference to a 'santo de piedra' who
gives us the most penetrating sketch of the paradox that is Don
Alvaro: '¿Qué es don Alvaro? Casi me apena creerle un hombre
honrado, un hombre puro; pero de una pureza enjuta; no puede
sonreír; parece que se le haya helado la sangre bajo la piedra de que
fue hecho' (I, p.161). The narrator, too, refers to his 'manos de
imagen'. Hard and cold to the end, Don Alvaro is almost certainly
intended by Miró to be the living version of the statue of Nuestro
Padre San Daniel, with which indeed Paulina herself compares him
more than once.

Lawyer, tutor, newspaper editor, amateur historian and
pseudo-intellectual, Don Amancio is the other leading layman in
Oleza's Carlist coterie and the secretary to the Carlist club, the
Círculo de Labradores. Miró's portrayal of him lacks the sombre
tints of that of Don Alvaro, but he cuts no more sympathetic a
figure. Physically unattractive and prematurely old, he too makes a
pitifully inadequate husband for the delicate and dreamy María
Fulgencia. Incapable, it seems, of consummating his marriage, he

has to suffer the humiliation of seeing himself replaced in his wife's affection by a teenage pupil.[9] As the leading voice of the clerical and Carlist party of Oleza, Don Amancio has been endowed by the author with the proprietorship and editorship of the weekly *El Clamor de la Verdad*, from whose columns he fulminates in bombastic prose studded with biblical references against the Liberal government in Madrid and the decline of traditional values. The pseudonym chosen for him is probably an echo of his political leanings, and the way in which he describes his role — a John the Baptist to Carlos VII — is Miró's ironic comment on his creature's absurd sense of self-importance, and perhaps by extension on the Carlists' chimerical expectations. A pedant and a plagiarist to boot, the outstanding characteristics of Don Amancio are his verbose and solemn utterances and his pompous manner; but his cultured speech hides a more serious fault: his constant and insidious denigration of those whose views he does not share, notably of Don Magín and the new Bishop. His oft-repeated phrase 'Oleza sigue huérfana' is a scarcely-veiled attack on the Bishop, whose lack of enthusiasm for those of Don Amancio's ilk the latter resents.

Don Cruz and Father Bellod regard don Amancio as a devout Catholic, a tireless worker, a selfless follower of legitimacy in his untiring devotion to the Carlist cause (though at the end his 'fracaso conyugal' leads to an uncharacteristic 'tibieza política'). But by using Monera the homeopath, the fifth member of the coterie, who is constantly made to feel inferior and who does not really share the religious and political fervours of his four companions, Miró craftily gives a different view of Don Amancio without describing him directly. We learn through Monera, piqued at the others' constant praise of Don Amancio, what the gossip-mongers have to say about

---

[9]The inference is based on Miró's description of María Fulgencia's bedroom after her marriage as being not just separate from that of her husband but as 'inocente' and 'dormitorio de candidez de virgen', and her bed as 'camita de soltera', and on the fact that the house is described as 'domicilio de célibe' and the lives of husband and wife as 'distantes'. According to Doña Purita the bride and groom had made a vow to live like brother and sister, which accords with Father Bellod's views on marriage.

him: that he uses the students at his school to copy out his legal documents for him; that he was making money hand over fist because he had not only his legal practice and his school, but also an honorarium from the town council for his writings on local history, which were in any case his uncle's work; that he received a stipend for acting as librarian in the Carlist club; and that he should be ashamed of accepting payments from all other fellow-Carlists for running his weekly paper. Evidently religion and Carlism are for Don Amancio no obstacle to amassing a fortune, a mercenary attitude which differentiates him from the self-denying Don Alvaro.

A rather different kind of Carlist is Cara-rajada, one of the characters about whose past we learn most but who remains a puzzling blend of sadism and sentimentality. The son of a Carlist fighter in the first war, Cara-rajada used to listen as a child to the tales of war recounted in his father's *tertulia*. When the Carlist conflict flares up again Cara-rajada secretly donates all his widowed mother's savings and joins the faction. Responsible for two horrendous murders and many other deaths besides, he himself suffers an appalling wound and a hideous disfigurement to his face. The experience of war also provokes a recrudescence of his child-hood epilepsy, which now manifests itself in violent seizures. He lives on the margins of society, full of resentment at the fate which has robbed him of his youthful dream of returning to Oleza from the war as a hero to claim the beautiful Paulina. Instead he has emerged mutilated and impoverished, shunned by some for his corpse-like and repulsive appearance and looked upon by others as a man possessed by the devil because of his epileptic fits. On the other hand Don Alvaro emerged unscathed, respected, and what was worse, was now claiming Paulina as his prize. It is through Paulina that Miró suggests that Cara-rajada is deserving of pity. In a scene reminiscent of another in the New Testament in which Jesus asks the Samaritan woman for a drink of water (St John 4:7), Paulina accedes to a similar request from Cara-rajada, and later she again takes pity, protecting him from the eager blows of the peasants. On each occasion, however, she has to make an enormous effort to overcome her natural repugnance at the ugliness and fervent utterances of Cara-rajada. Yet there is more to Cara-rajada than his physical deformity, and indeed the latter seems indicative of an inner degeneracy. The repugnance which he provokes is not due solely to his ghastly appearance, for Miró presents him as a depraved being, morally and mentally. His irrational hatred of Don Alvaro, explicable now in terms of envy, predates his own injury; he hated him from the very first time he set eyes on him, and his hatred, which had provoked him into committing a savagely brutal and callous crime during the war, now, upon Don Alvaro's reappearance, sparks off an inner frenzy that makes him stalk the newcomer day and night in an obsessive search to vent his frustrations and despair by exacting revenge on the man who has made him feel inferior and whose popular acclamation he envies. The callousness of Cara-rajada is not just in his crimes but also in the way he relates them without any sign of remorse. Significantly, Don Magín suggests that Cara-rajada is the victim not only of his own unfulfilled expectations and consequent bitterness, but also of the hatred and barbarity emanating from the Carlist ideology and the stories of the guerrilla fighters which so excited him as a child. His depravity, Miró appears to be suggesting, is to be laid at the door of a movement that romanticizes and condones the most hideous crimes carried out in the name of a political and religious ideology. Don Magín's plea to Cara-rajada, that 'tu heroísmo puede principiar ahora, y no envidiando a don Alvaro ni maquinando venganzas' (I, p.161), is in the end ignored, and in his frenzied attempts to whip up the mob from the poor quarter of Oleza against the Carlists, Cara-rajada finds himself derided and pursued by his former neighbours, and as he flees is caught in the surging waters of the bursting river. 'No soy ningún monstruo', he had earlier entreated Don Magín (I, p.159); yet as the swirling river claims his life his final and chilling thought is to curse his protector and benefactor.

The five major female characters in the novels offer perhaps greater diversity than do their male counterparts, though the theme of frustration and regret is if anything more marked, for all suffer from a lack of fulfilment in some way or other. Paulina is a passive victim: of the social circle in which she belongs, of her father's good intentions, and even of her own impressionable nature. Kind, beautiful, and bright, accustomed to wandering as a child and young woman in the joyful fields of the family estate, once married she has to suffer the constant vigilance of a bitchy and cheerless sister-in-law and of an austere and cold-hearted husband twice her age; and worse, she has to suffer virtual imprisonment in a house as gloomy as her husband. But Paulina does not protest; indeed she seems all too ready to let herself be victimized. She desperately wants to visit her dying father but is unable to summon the courage to go against her husband's wishes and even defends his attitude before the shocked maidservant Jimena. Whether Paulina truly loves her husband or not, Miró prefers not to say. To begin with she is excited by the prospect of marriage. Her childish innocence even anticipates the pleasure of gaining a new sister through her marriage. She believes herself to be in love with Don Alvaro, but Miró hints that it might not be a spontaneous love: 'Amaba a don Alvaro, y le amaba tan hondamente que se extraviaba en una niebla temerosa, y hasta creía amarle por obediencia, sin recibir ningún mandato' (I, p.172). Paulina's enthusiasm, her 'delicioso sobresalto', is like that of a child about to set out on a new and exciting adventure. The thought of marriage, of children, is an enjoyable prospect. But she loves Don Alvaro as a husband-figure rather than as an individual whose personality and company she likes: '[...] el nombre, el recuerdo y el anuncio del amado le prometían mayores bienes y dulzuras que su misma presencia' (I, p.173). Indeed in his presence her excitement finds no fulfilment; on the contrary, Don Alvaro's severe comportment makes her 'contenida y callada'.

We learn little of Paulina's own feelings during the first years of her marriage, and the full extent of the harsh, unloving marital situation imposed by Don Alvaro's aversion to any natural expression of feeling becomes apparent only in Volume II. But towards the end of Volume I Miró includes two brief incidents in quick succession which act as pointers and whose full significance will be crystallized in the sequel. In the first incident Paulina is looking across the street from her window and smiling. Elvira enters unnoticed, and Miró describes what she sees through the window standing behind Paulina: Máximo, the Countess's brother, on the balcony of the Lóriz palace holding his new-born godchild in his arms and rocking him to sleep with a lullaby. Don Alvaro of course is never seen showing any tenderness towards his son. The second incident follows immediately when Paulina is urged by Elvira to go to confession. In the silence of the empty church she hears the doors being locked and suddenly experiences the sensation of being buried alive. She turns to the staring eyes of the statue of San Daniel and sees 'un don Alvaro espantoso' (I, p.274). Miró would appear to be suggesting that Paulina's subconscious, if not her conscious, mind has sensed Don Alvaro's role as ever-vigilant keeper of her whole being. The two incidents are of course subtly inter-related, although there is scarcely a hint to this effect. Their full significance becomes apparent only in Volume II, if, that is, the reader recalls the relevant lines of narrative from the earlier volume.

The reappearance of Máximo, many years later during Holy Week, is used by Miró to give us a more profound insight into Paulina's mind and emotions. The warmth of his manner, of his eyes and his lips, makes a deep impact upon her, making her wonder what marriage to such a man would have been like. For her, it is clear, Máximo represents a missed opportunity of happiness:'"Ya llevaríamos diecisiete años casados desde entonces; diecisiete años ..." Y todo esto voló de su frente, por el horizonte del Olivar de aquellos días deshojados, sin sobresaltos de casada perfecta. No se había complacido en otro amor, sino en otro matrimonio, otro matrimonio que le parecía referido a distinta mujer' (II, p.208). The following day Paulina watches the Good Friday procession from her balcony. She feels it is her duty to fix her gaze on her husband, processing alongside the dead Christ. But her mind is very much on Máximo, who is watching her from the balcony on the other side of the street. She feels his warm gaze upon her 'como una luz', and cannot resist the urge to return that gaze, 'y ella se vio delante de todos, sola, iluminada calientemente, como si toda la procesión del Entierro de Cristo le hubiese acercado las velas para sorprenderle los pensamientos' (II, p.230). The representation of Christ's Passion becomes for Paulina the representation of a

forbidden passion.[10] Because of her thoughts she feels guilty, and
this guilt, though certainly not labelled as such by Miró, is rendered
symbolically by reference to the dead Christ and by association with
the popular perception of San Daniel as the accuser of inconstant
women: 'Y continuaban las hileras temblorosas de luces amarillas.
Cirios y luto. A lo último, el resplandor helado del sepulcro de
cristal, y bajo el sudario fosforescente de riquezas, el Señor muerto,
el Señor que se volvió para mirar a Paulina, lo mismo que la noche
que le tuvo miedo a Nuestro Padre San Daniel' (II, p.231). Paulina's
escape into a dreamworld of love is some indication of the harsh
imprisonment that is her marriage, but her unhappiness is in any
case more than hinted at in a host of other detail. 'En casa siempre
llora la mamá', says seven-year-old Pablo (II, p.90), and indeed
sollozo and *sollozar* are words often associated with Paulina.
Dominated by her husband and sister-in-law, she remains passive
almost to the end. She has her son sent as a boarder to the Jesuit
school against her will and later allows herself to be deprived of
attending his graduation ceremony. Curiously, Paulina begins to act
positively only when her son's close friendship with María
Fulgencia is discovered, though this may be seen to be a result of
Elvira's disgrace. The latter not only means there is one enemy
fewer to contend with, but also has the effect of undermining
Alvaro's authority and his hold over Paulina and Pablo, because
Alvaro and Elvira have always defended the same point of view.
Perhaps, too, Paulina sees in her son's adolescent love for María
Fulgencia a reflection of her own adolescent love for Máximo. At
any rate, whatever Miró's own perception of Paulina's change was,
there is no doubt that by the end of the novel Paulina and Pablo
have achieved a degree of emancipation from Alvaro, even if only
because the latter is a broken man who can no longer resist his
wife's and son's wish to go and live in El Olivar. But Miró leaves
the question of happiness wide open. Paulina goes off to El Olivar

---

[10]On the literary ancestry of the religious/secular dichotomy of the Passion
see Jane Yvonne Tillier, 'Passion Poetry in the *Cancioneros*', *Bulletin of
Hispanic Studies*, 62 (1985), 65–78.

in search of happiness; whether she finds it or not does not fall within the confines of the novel. Her life is one more symbol of every human being's search for fulfilment in the midst of tribulation and disappointment.

Doña Corazón Motos is another victim of Don Daniel Egea's good intentions. Secretly in love with Don Daniel, she is pressurized by him into marrying an absolute cad whose kindest act towards his wife is to leave her a widow. In her widowed state Doña Corazón devotes herself to running her pastry shop, to receiving her many friends, and to watching the town of Oleza with her kindly eyes. But just as Don Daniel was blind to Doña Corazón's undeclared love for him, so the widow is blind to Don Vicente Grifol's undeclared love for her, yet another of Miró's variations on the theme of unfulfilled happiness. Everyone likes Doña Corazón, except those who, like Elvira, Father Bellod, or Don Amancio, are guided by a false notion of what constitutes virtue. Doña Corazón is a simple woman, embarrassed because Father Bellod discovers that she incubates poultry eggs in her bosom. She enjoys the company of Don Jeromillo and Don Magín, but is unsettled by the latter because he speaks a language full of insinuations. Although naturally diffident and circumspect, when Don Magín tells her of Don Daniel's consuming sadness because of the continued absence of his daughter, she plucks up enough courage to go to Don Alvaro's house to plead for Paulina to be allowed to go to her father. But her straightforward honesty and simplicity are no match for the crafty and malevolent Elvira. Doña Corazón is shocked and reduced to tears by the spiteful and vicious accusations against many of the inhabitants of Oleza. She is too kindly and self-effacing to react with indignation, and merely cowers in the face of the other woman's venomous tongue. But if Doña Corazón has never learnt to stand up to others, she does not begrudge others her help when help is needed. She it is who looks after Don Daniel during his illness and who dresses Don Magín's wound and acts as a nurse during his convalescence. Incapable of an unkind word, she has, according to Don Magín, 'entrañas de azucenas' (II, p.175). In Volume II she is into old age, and, confined to a chair, has to limit herself to receiving her friends at home. In the end she comes to personify the passage of time and the passing of an age: 'En el regazo de Doña Corazón y entre sus manos pulidas y perfumadas de sebillo de bergamota se dormían los años viejos de Oleza, y a la vez rodaban las mudanzas de los tiempos' (II, p.381).

If Cara-rajada is the most depraved character in the novel, then the most odious must surely be Elvira Galindo. Her unpleasant nature, her inability to find anything good in other people, indeed her constant insinuations of depraved and immoral conduct, are some indication not only of her own vile nature but also of her embittered and frustrated self. Like her brother, she is incapable of expressing warmth and affection, and for her too, religion has become a justification for condemning any manifestation of pleasure, joy, or tenderness. Meanness, hypocrisy, and sadism add to her unsavoury character. She hoards food and refuses to give any dessert to the maidservants, even accusing one of them of gluttony for keeping fig-bread in her room; but she herself secretly indulges in sweetmeats which she keeps locked away in her chest of drawers. She takes obvious delight in announcing to the seven-year-old Pablo that he is to be shut up in the Jesuit school and in reminding him day after day of the horrible prospect of losing his freedom. She also frightens him with supernatural tales and takes pleasure in his punishment. Pablo's comment on this particular occasion is a good example of Miró's way of letting us see into Doña Elvira's character: 'Y esa tía Elvira no se ríe como ellas. No puede. ¡Pero me miraba riéndose cuando me castigaron!' (II, p.228). Elvira's outstanding characteristic, however, is her venomous tongue. She derives sadistic satisfaction from spreading calumnies and insinuations about those who have the simple capacity to enjoy life that she lacks. No sooner has she met Paulina than she expresses her dislike of her father whom she has not yet met but been spying on through a window. Her treatment of the well-intentioned Doña Corazón is once again cruel to the point of sadism. Her vilification of the seventeen-year-old Purita suggests a deep-seated envy born of repressed sexuality. And it is envy of her sister-in-law's beauty and the public's fascination with her that makes her contrive Paulina's

confinement at home. Her frustrated sexuality eventually comes out
into the open in a sudden and unexpected manner. Impelled by a
mad jealousy caused by Pablo's predilection for María Fulgencia
and his rejection of her, she gives vent to a frenzied sexual attack
upon her nephew. The incident happens very quickly and Miró does
not dwell on it; but he leaves us in no doubt whatever about the
sexual nature of the attack: it is virtually a rape scene in reverse.
While this is an unexpected climax to Elvira's sexual obsession, her
latent sexuality has been hinted at by Miró all along, not only in her
imaginary detection of sexual promiscuity and depravity in others
but also in brief and telling passages whose significance has tended
to pass unnoticed: 'Paulina sonreía, estremeciéndosele apasionada-
mente los pechos. Elvira se puso a su espalda, y aspiró el perfume
de su respiración. Le pareció sentirla como hombre' (I, p.270). The
hint of an abnormal sexuality is there, even if Miró prefers not to
elaborate. Her physique as described by Miró is also suggestive: tall
and bony, with a voice full of passion and a frothy mouth, and flat-
breasted in contrast to Paulina's shapely female figure. Her constant
attacks on those women of whom she does not approve and her
irrational accusations of licentiousness betray an obsession with
carnal sins which is portrayed as indicative of a warped sense of
virtue. She sees rampant sexuality all around her — even in a statue
during a Holy Week procession — but her religious outlook
prevents her from recognizing it in herself. Her relish in telling
prurient anecdotes about other people and her savage character
assassination (her venomous tongue is at work even in church) are
symptoms of a misconceived religious philosophy which holds
sexual repression to be virtuous. Miró suggests that Doña Elvira's
religion (which in the eyes of Don Cruz and others is both the
explanation and justification of her censure of loose morals) is not
only harmful but lacks ethical transcendence, being reduced to mere
ritual and perhaps even self-indulgence: 'La confesión de Elvira fue
un diálogo apasionado y profuso' (I, p.272). It is not even a
consolation for her own lack of a channel through which to satisfy
her sensuality. It is a sex-substitute that makes her sanctimonious,
sadistic and sexually warped. She has neither true religious feeling

nor human warmth; her only outlet is her poisoned tongue. Perhaps Miró's clearest statement on Elvira is to be found in Don Daniel's untypically shrewd assessment (quoted earlier) to the effect that her constant denunciation of sin has contaminated her with its moral stain.

Spinsterhood is the one characteristic that Purita Canci shares with Elvira Galindo. In every other respect she is her opposite. Purita's spinsterhood is partly the result of her own family circumstances and partly the consequence of the closed society of Oleza, which, because of her attractiveness and outgoing personality, considers her 'demasiado libre' to make a good wife. Being an orphan living in an aunt's house she is compelled to reject suitors — who are in any case discouraged — until such time as her two cousins have married. Don Magín considers that Purita would have made a good mother; her enforced spinsterhood is therefore in his view a tragedy, and in fact we do know that she has a generous and self-sacrificing nature. She it is who takes on the task of looking after Don Vicente Grifol day and night on his death-bed and later goes off to look after her young nephews. Yet far from being resentful of her fate or full of self-pity Purita retains her cheerfulness and vivacity: 'Lo que pudo acabar en un gemido, se abrió en un alboroto de risa' (II, p.177). Like her greatest admirer, Don Magín, Purita stands out as one of the few characters in the novel in whom there is no duplicity, no hypocrisy, no pretence. Not dominated by the concept of the naked body as sinful, she delights in the beauty of her figure, likes what she sees in the mirror and is not ashamed to say so. Doña Elvira and her puritanical friends regard Purita as a slut who parades herself naked at night for the benefit of the Count of Lóriz. The Jesuits, too, regard her with disapproval, as a source of provocation of sinful desires. Yet Miró leaves us in no doubt that Purita is as pure as her name indicates. Don Magín, whom he has depicted as a shrewd judge of character, even if not an altogether impartial one, says of her: 'Yo la proclamo la más casta y la más virgen de todas las solteras de la diócesis' (II, p.154). Nor is Purita in any sense irreligious. Miró makes it clear that she participates in the religious life of Oleza as much as do her denigrators: like

Paulina, she belongs to the *cofradía de la samaritana* (a mark of approval from Miró, much attracted by this biblical figure, but not from Elvira, for whom the Samaritan is nothing but a slut), and is secretary to many religious associations. What is distinct about her is her positive attitude to life. She knows that men find her attractive and rewards her admirers with joyful laughter, undaunted by the Jesuits' displeasure or the puritans' censure. Perhaps the quality that comes through most powerfully in Miró's characterization of her is her high spirits and enjoyment of life. Her vivacious and joyful disposition contrasts sharply with the gloomy and repressive atmosphere that afflicts much of respectable society in Oleza.

The fifth female character with a major role is María Fulgencia, who shares with Paulina the circumstance of an unhappy marriage and the concomitant attraction of another man, in her case of the youthful Pablo. But unlike Paulina, she has not had a happy childhood, and it is the incidents of her childhood (the strange resurrection of her father and the death of her sister) that are perhaps meant to explain in part her somewhat baffling behaviour. Miró has conceived her as a latter-day mystic, although childish and naïve, but the real nature of her pseudo-mystical impulses remains obscure. Like Elvira and Cara-rajada she evinces deviant behaviour, but in her case it is comparatively harmless, except that it leads her into a disastrous marriage that remains unconsummated. Brought up in isolation, her impressionable nature leads to her teenage infatuation with her cousin Mauricio, who treats her as a plaything. Her extreme sensibility makes her take refuge in mystical pursuits and the bizarre devotion to the statue of the Angel, in what Miró hints is psychological displacement. In a sense therefore what we have in María Fulgencia is another case of religion gone awry. The Dean, her guardian, suspects that her devotion to the Angel may not be what it seems: 'El Angel, a pesar de su androginismo, ¿no se revelaría para la huérfana con un espiritual contorno y hechizo masculino?' (II, p.138), and as if to confirm his suspicions El Angel is quickly identified in María Fulgencia's mind with Pablo Galindo. In the convent of the Order of the Visitation María Fulgencia gives herself up to the spiritual life with the intensity of a mystic, much to the perplexity of the abbess; but she also brings gaiety to the life of the young novitiates, much to the chagrin of the Mother *Clavaria*. María Fulgencia's interest in matters sexual, even if clothed in mystical trappings, unsettles convent life, for the cloistered women of La Visitación find a novel excitement in the appearance of the young Hussar Mauricio, whom they imagine, encouraged by María Fulgencia's mystical visions, as an archangel visiting them in their cells at night. María Fulgencia's attachment to the pair of turtle doves she brings with her to the convent is another hint of the nature of her problem, and the *Clavaria*'s malevolent action in killing the male bird (symbolic of the rupture of the love bond) provokes her stormy abandonment of the religious life. Her marriage to the old-looking and abstemious Don Amancio does not of course satisfy her hankering after the loving relationship she has never enjoyed. Her affair with Pablo is intense but pure, or rather her love for him is like her love for the turtle doves, a need to love. Cousin Mauricio had not responded to a sentiment that was part profane, part mystical; but the younger, more innocent Pablo is still at an age when profane love and religious sentiment blend into a feeling of elation. It is, however, a human, not divine, passion, though not a sinful one. Miró deliberately contrasts the love between María Fulgencia and Pablo with the debauchery of Diego, Tonda, and the maidservants. But if the former is a pure love, it is nonetheless a prohibited love, an echo perhaps of Paradise, with a Spanish lemon substituted for the biblical apple (*10*, p.242). María Fulgencia knows this, as her reaction on being discovered by Diego proves. Yet now she serenely accepts the loss of Pablo and the loss of happiness without making any attempt to disguise the truth, as she calmly informs her husband and as she later admits in her letter to Paulina: 'Y no quise fingir, porque él y yo solos, sin pensar en los demás, no caímos en ninguna vergüenza; pero pensar en los otros hasta tener que engañarles era ya sentirse desnudos' (II, p.367). The reference to Genesis contained in the last two words accords with the concept of sin suggested by Miró in this novel: sinfulness is an awareness of sin, a sense of shame. María Fulgencia's role becomes clearer. For Miró, her love for Pablo is not sinful; the sinfulness of their relationhip is created by others, and it is this overbearing concept of sin that destroys the possibility of happiness.

Like María Fulgencia, Pablo does not have an entirely normal or happy childhood, owing to the strained relations and austere existence of the Galindo household. Characterized as a sensitive boy fighting for normality, he compares his home with the relaxed and happy atmosphere in the Lóriz household. As a young boy Pablo does not conform to the wishes of his father and aunt: he leaves home surreptitiously at siesta time, joins Don Magín, and together they roam the Bishop's palace. Pablo's spirit of independence and his friendship with the rival clerical circle, resented by his father and aunt and their friends, lead to his internment in the Jesuit school on his eighth birthday. What little else we learn of Pablo's childhood is achieved largely through memories, though a few aspects stand out: he much prefers El Olivar to his father's house, he identifies with his mother's side of the family rather than his father's, and he detests his aunt and his father's Carlist friends but enjoys the company of Don Magín. The actual process of Pablo growing up until he reaches his final year in school is not directly depicted. We pass from his childhood to his adolescence, just as we pass from his birth in Volume I to his eighth birthday in Volume II. The intervening eight years are not covered in any detail except for intermittent retrospective glances. But Miró includes enough in passing references and sketches to suggest his gloomy existence at 'Jesús', broken only by an occasional excursion, such as that to the Lórizs' home during the Holy Week processions, and by the holidays spent at home largely at his mother's side. What is also clear is that Pablo loves his mother, heartily detests his aunt, and feels no affection whatever for his father, whom he fears and identifies with his aunt rather than with his mother. At sixteen Pablo is depicted as still boyish, sensitive both to religious emotion, particularly during the Holy Week liturgy, and to an awakening sensuality. His interest in the pictures of nuns and virgin martyrs suggests a sexual awareness showing through the layers of religious inculcation. It is his romantic affair with *la monja* that takes him from childhood to adulthood. Pablo and María Fulgencia are both lonely adolescents, Pablo by now having lost all his schoolfriends. He is seventeen, or so he says, she cannot be more than some months older, and her girlish immaturity and flightiness make her seem younger. Their romantic attachment is on one level an adolescent infatuation, but on another it is clearly the result of each one's unhappy circumstances. Pablo's infatuation is explicable in that his meeting with a kindred spirit is a means of compensating for his difficult home life. Also, María Fulgencia is entirely different from the other — lewd, coarse, and nasty — inhabitants of Don Amancio's house and school, and that makes him identify more with her. The more repugnant he finds Diego and the others, the more attractive he finds the delicate and ethereal María Fulgencia. His experience beside her seems more aesthetic than sexual. There is, certainly, an element of sensuality, but, as Miró presents it, it is bound up less with sex than with the delicate fragrance of the lemon tree and the jasmine. It is a youthful, idealistic, and pure love, one that causes him delight though mixed with some feelings of guilt, not because he sees his relationship with María Fulgencia as sinful but because he has achieved happiness while others continue to suffer. And it is this thought that makes him take a detour to the Bishop's palace while on his way to see his beloved: 'Cuando María Fulgencia le besara bajo su limonero, él podría decirse: "Pero yo estuve en casa del que sufre, y sufrí"' (II, p.352). What Pablo learns from his experience is that he does not live by himself upon an island, that his happiness is the source of others' unhappiness: 'Su deleite y su amor [...] eran desgracia para otros' (II, p.359). He can even begin to feel compassion for his discredited aunt. In common with so many other characters Pablo has to experience the sense of loss, of a promise of happiness unfulfilled; but his horizons, unlike theirs, can stretch outwards as he contemplates the train that departs for faraway places.

Major Characters (2)

In a novel in which religion and clerical influence play such a central role it is not surprising that many of the characters should be in holy orders. The number of characters that belong to the clergy is well in excess of twenty, but five in particular have been singled out for more extended treatment. They are, in order of first mention, Don Cruz, Padre Bellod, Don Jeromillo, Don Magín and the Bishop.

Don Cruz is perhaps less fully drawn than the other clerical characters; at any rate we are not directly told as much about him as about the other major clerical figures. As penitentiary canon in Oleza cathedral he is a leading ecclesiastical figure and considered by many of the faithful, but especially by his constant companion Don Amancio, to be the natural successor to the deceased bishop. Whether he himself aspires to the mitre Miró does not state in so many words, but the inference must be that he does. In public Don Cruz denies all interest in being elevated, but on the other hand does nothing positive to discourage the campaign in his favour; when the official list of candidates is made public he rushes off to tell his promoter; when the news of the appointment explodes throughout Oleza, just as the commission in support of Don Cruz's candidature is about to leave, he and *Alba Longa* retire crestfallen; and eighteen years later, following the death of Bishop Céspedes, he expresses regret that no one now demands an appointment to the vacant see. These various touches suggest that Miró wants us to understand that Don Cruz does harbour ambitions and that his humility and his disclaimers are a pose. Because he hardly ever appears on his own, and because in the company of others he has a tendency to express himself cryptically, often by biblical quotation and allusion to ecclesiastical writings, it is not easy to know what he

thinks, but this is part and parcel of Miró's characterization of him.
Leader of his Carlist coterie, his ambitions nevertheless make him
politically cautious; thus he stays away from the reception for Don
Alvaro at the Círculo de Labradores but ensures that the apolitical
Don Daniel is dragged along. Manipulating other people's lives is
one of his major functions, and not necessarily for their greater
happiness. There is a hint that he has had a hand in arranging the
marriage between Don Alvaro and Paulina, and he is certainly
instrumental in finding a house for the newly-weds and encouraging
the separation of father and daughter as well as keeping Doña
Corazón away. It is Don Cruz who gives Pablo his name, and it is
largely through his influence and his tacit condemnation of Pablo's
friendship with Don Magín that the young boy is interned in 'Jesús'.
Although never carrying his austerity to the extremes of Father
Bellod, he is nevertheless a sombre and somewhat austere figure
too. He warns Don Daniel against his boyish enthusiasms, even
against becoming too enthralled by his daughter, and again he
subtly discredits Paulina's love for her son by a tendentious citation
of St Augustine. Pompous and sententious, he and *Alba Longa* share
cryptic exchanges that reveal their hostility towards the new
occupant of the episcopal palace, while his *tertulias* are usually full
of veiled, censorious comments on other people. He even makes
cruel fun of Monera and treats the distressed mother of Cara-rajada
with harshness. Although Miró has not characterized him through
direct description, indirectly we are given to understand that Don
Cruz's view of religion is essentially negative and bookish. He has a
learned mind but a cold heart. The anecdote he tells in the presence
of Don Daniel and Paulina of the mother who steadfastly refused to
forgive her son even though he implored forgiveness on her
deathbed is obviously meant by Miró to reveal this particular
character's unchristian concept of virtue.

Yet it is not Don Cruz but Father Bellod who entertains the
truly fearful concept of religion. The most austere of the clerics in
the novel, he takes religious austerity to a quite frightening pitch.
Even harmless pleasures of the senses, like the taste of delicacies
and the fragrance of flowers, hold nothing for him. He is as harsh

with himself as he is with others. He refuses to use soap or even water to shave, and seems almost to derive satisfaction from drawing his own blood. He treats the younger priests in his church of San Bartolomé with military discipline, imposing a strict regime of physical exercise as well as of poverty, extreme simplicity and privation; so much so that the priests, sacristans, acolytes, and others who share Father Bellod's abode in San Bartolomé jump with joy upon hearing that their superior has been promoted to the rectorship of Nuestro Padre San Daniel. Yet the aspect of Father Bellod's religious austerity that Miró emphasizes is his obsession with chastity and his loathing of anything to do with sex: 'enfurecido de castidad', in Miró's telling phrase (I, p.241). His most prized virtue is virginity, not just in himself but in others. 'Su confesionario hacía estremecer los más limpios corazones femeninos', we are told (I, p.74); and he is described as 'mastín del rebaño blanco de las vírgenes de Oleza' (II, p.156). He is filled with anger when he considers the indignities brought by marriage; if people must get married the least they can do is to show their love for each other by practising continence. He even discourages the locutory hour at the convent because he considers it a danger for the nuns, and looks upon the new Recreo Benéfico, despite its charitable aims, as a worm-hole because it holds fêtes and dances. His favourite religious legends are those that tell of the triumph of virgins over dangers and temptations, especially where martyrdom is involved. Indeed he even seems to find some kind of satisfaction in showing Pablo the descriptions of the gruesome tortures imposed on martyrs, which he glosses using the present tense, as if it were a continuing phenomenon, not forgetting to mention the 'ultrajes y suplicios de muchas vírgenes cristianas' (II, p.326), which Pablo is nevertheless not allowed to see. We are forced to the conclusion that Miró is depicting a cleric whose religious austerity verges on perversion. Indeed the novelist himself on this occasion abandons his usual reticence to make the perversion abundantly clear when, referring to the priest's feverish turning over of the pages of the *Acta Martyrum*, he writes: '[...] buscaba precipitándose encima del folio, y su ojo abierto relucía de delirio algolágnico' (II, p.326). Father Bellod may delude himself into believing that heaven is populated by resplendent virgins, but his own repressed sexuality, of which his exhortations to others to preserve their virginity are but a symptom, finds a perverted outlet in his sadistic treatment of animals. Not content with setting traps for the rats in his church and disposing of them forthwith, he slowly and methodically sets about burning them alive while listening to their screams: first the whiskers, then the muzzle, then the ears, 'y les dejaba los ojos para lo último porque le divertía su mirada de lumbrecillas lívidas' (I, p.77). He then grants his victims a temporary respite, only to return to his gruesome task by bashing their heads in with the incense tongs. For him the rats are representations of sin, and the destruction of the hideous and pestilential animals is akin to the destruction of the sin that corrupts human beings. Nor is this the only cruelty perpetrated by Father Bellod on animals. He grabs a frightened dog by the scruff of the neck and hurls it against the railings; he kills a cat by giving it a sponge to eat and watching it swell in its stomach; and he advises the nuns to boil María Fulgencia's pet turtle doves. But the most revealing act of sadism is the treatment he metes out to the rook in the Círculo de Labradores, which is a precise reflection of the hideous method of torture inflicted on martyrs which he had earlier described to Pablo. At this point Father Bellod's perverted mind cannot be held in doubt. For even though Miró does not directly condemn him at any stage, his characterization of him leaves us in no doubt that something is very seriously wrong; and what is wrong of course is Bellod's concept of religion, a religion based not on love and understanding but on repression, on threats, and on the obsession with carnal sins.

If Don Cruz and Padre Bellod are to be counted amongst the most influential clerics in the ecclesiastical hierarchy of Oleza, Don Jeromillo is at the opposite pole. Chaplain to the nuns of the Order of St Francis de Sales (La Visitación), he commands affection but not respect, much less fear: everyone calls him by the diminutive instead of using the more formal Don Jerónimo. Even the nuns tell him off, if mildly, for his clumsy ways and indecorous expletives. He is of peasant stock (traditionally a common provenance of the

Spanish priesthood), still obvious in his rustic speech and total lack of sophistication. 'Carne rural y alma de Dios', as the narrator calls him (II, p.139), Don Jeromillo is a simple soul, so unworldly that even the nuns' small-talk disconcerts him. He is something of a dunce too, makes mistakes at prayer, and stands in childish awe of some of the stories in the Bible, such as the Flood. His one weakness is Doña Corazón's cooking and larder full of goodies which he finds irresistible and which he regards with a mixture of reverence and delight. The prospect of the yearly visit to Doña Corazón's table on the eve of St Peter and St Paul fills him with an excited sense of anticipation, and the sudden announcement of just such a feast on the day of Paulina's wedding leaves him so agitated that he knocks over a ceremonial candlestick in the chapel. His simplicity, his naïvety, the total absence of duplicity in his person ('la más grande inocencia' according to Purita: II, p.177), make him an endearing character, but he lacks the awareness and therefore the psychological complexity of his close friend and protector Don Magín. He is deeply attached to Don Magín and feels great admiration for him, yet he clearly does not know what to make of the latter's humanistic learning. His whole world is in the stories of the Bible, which he does not even aspire to understand, and in what he sees in Oleza: his simple mind does not let him move beyond these limited horizons. For all his simple-mindedness Don Jeromillo is warm-hearted, a quality singularly lacking in Don Cruz and Father Bellod. When Don Magín is shot, he takes over, much to his own surprise, and asks that the wounded man be carried to his apartment and laid on his bed. The privations he has to suffer are compensated by his importance as protector of Don Magín in a sudden and ingenious reversal of roles. For a while he becomes the centre of attention as everyone of note in Oleza sets foot in his modest residence. There he receives the Countess and assists the Bishop at Mass, and for once is able to feel important and the equal of people in whose presence he always felt inferior. But once Don Magín has recovered and returned to his parish, Don Jeromillo reverts to being the humble, diffident, barely-noticed chaplain of La Visitación. Don Jeromillo is the clerical equivalent of Don Daniel: both are simple-minded

traditionalists, but neither is an austere kill-joy. Just as Don Daniel
is no political fanatic, so Don Jeromillo is no religious bigot. He is
presented by Miró as a picture of childlike innocence, unsophisti-
cated in his religion and in his attitudes, but at the same time
generous and receptive to the simple joys of life. Doña Corazón,
another simple and warm-hearted individual, prefers the company
of Don Jeromillo at her table to that of Don Magín, for all the
latter's intelligence and wit, because Don Jeromillo's uncomplicated
view of life has the capacity to reassure.

Yet it is very clearly Don Magín who is closest to Miró's heart
and who, in contrast to Father Bellod, embodies the acceptable face
of Catholicism. Promoted to parish priest of San Bartolomé after
Father Bellod's transfer to San Daniel, Don Magín is in some ways
the odd man out in the clerical society of Oleza. Not for him the
austerities of Father Bellod: considered lax in his priestly habits, he
is much given to perambulating the streets and to inhaling the
sundry fragrances of the town, culinary and botanical. For Oleza
Don Magín is a paradox: a sensual man, yet one whose sins are
unknown. Everyone expected him to be sinful because of the way he
was, yet no one knew of any sin that he had committed. At the end
of the novel the narrator comments: ' no se le perdonaba la paradoja
de que, siendo según era, fuese puro' (II, p.378). There is an
unusual sensuousness in Don Magín, one that makes him peculiarly
sensitive to life's pleasures — especially those of an olfactory kind
such as the scent of flowers, incense, fine tobaccos, or freshly-baked
bread — yet accompanied by a complete detachment from sin. If
Father Bellod is obsessed with sin and penance, Don Magín seems
almost blissfully unaware of either. Indeed the extent of Oleza's
ridiculous concept of sexual perversity is, according to Don Magín,
that Doña Purita can be thought to sin not just in Spanish but in
French and Italian as well because she listens to Don Roger speaking in those foreign tongues. He also displays a good deal of
common sense in areas where others do not: he realizes, for
example, the source of María Fulgencia's and the young nuns'
pseudo-mystical excitement and arranges for Mauricio to be sent on
his way, at the same time revealing his scepticism of the miraculous

powers of relics. Don Magín has an air of opulence about him — symbolized in part by his fine Genoese umbrella — and is described, first by Father Bellod and later by others, as having the appearance of a cardinal. Yet this so-called cardinal has no professional ambitions whatsoever and is adamant in his refusal of a canonry with which the Bishop seeks to reward him; instead he accepts it for another fellow-cleric suffering from the harsh rule of Father Bellod. His undoubted influence at the episcopal palace is due precisely to the fact that, unlike so many commissions that visit the Bishop asking for favours, he seeks nothing for himself but looks after the interests of others. It is evident that the Bishop appreciates Don Magín's humane character right from the start, impressed by the latter's insistence on halting the inaugural procession while he fetches an infirm and elderly chaplain whose pleas are being ignored by those present. Don Magín is heartily detested by the Carlist coterie because he refuses to conform to their views, keeps company of which they do not approve, such as the Lórizs and Purita, and appears to favour the latter-day Oleza of the Nuevo Casino and other non-Carlist, non-Jesuit-approved enterprises. By contrast he is singled out by the Bishop for his good work: 'De Don Magín podemos tomar enseñanza algunos religiosos', he says rather pointedly in the presence of his arch-detractors Don Cruz and Don Amancio (I, p.167). Miró leaves us in no doubt that Don Magín is the most generous, most caring cleric in Oleza. He is the only one who tries to help Cara-rajada, spiritually and materially; he is the one who comes to the aid of the elderly priest El Abuelo, and gives him lodging in his own house; he is the only one who takes to visiting Don Daniel to keep him company in his new and lonely existence. And when he is lying on the ground wounded and bleeding, his concern is not for himself but for the distraught Don Jeromillo. Don Magín seems, too, the only cleric who remembers the deprived inhabitants of the city and visits the poor quarter of San Ginés to talk to them, to listen to their woes, even to arbitrate in their disputes and plead on their behalf before the municipal authorities for the rescission of the fines imposed on them because their children steal fruit from the trees of rich landowners. Whereas others, including Don Cruz, denounce them, Don Magín protects them. And as friend and protector he is regarded by the people, both in life and in death, for he is the one on whom they call for consolation in their final hours. Don Magín's visit to the Arrabal de San Ginés, his sharing of the lives of the underprivileged for a few hours, of their problems and tragedies and even of their prickly pears — not at all his favourite fruit — is not something that he relishes. It goes against his natural sensibilities: the poverty and the filth he finds repugnant. Yet he returns year after year. It seems certain that Miró has intended an implicit comparison between Don Magín's concern for the welfare of people and Don Cruz's and Father Bellod's concern for religious etiquette; and beyond the comparison of fictional characters there is the wider confrontation of two different concepts of religion. I shall be returning to this question in the final chapter, but for the moment we may note that Don Magín does not use religion to sermonize people. He uses his common sense, his deep understanding of human nature and sometimes even his natural indignation, as is the case over the enforced separation of Don Daniel and Paulina, referring to which he tells Doña Corazón:

> —Iba usted a decirme que cuando Nuestro Señor lo permite, por algo será. Y Nuestro Señor no permite las cosas por algo; eso lo hace un Don Cruz o un Don Amancio. Somos nosotros los que permitimos todo suspirando: ¡Sea lo que Dios quiera! (I, p.209)

Don Magín's indignation at Don Daniel's abandonment by his in-laws is dictated not by religion but by the natural reaction of a warm-hearted individual. Similarly, his anger at the brutal nature of Cara-rajada's crime is tempered by the realization of the motive underlying the crime and of Cara-rajada's need not for sermonizing but for reintegration. His interview with this unsavoury character is a remarkable example of psychological diagnosis.

Don Magín's religion is the expression of his personality, and not the other way around. Far from using his moral rectitude as a stick with which to beat other people, Don Magín accepts the weaknesses of human nature and does not think of his priestly duties as consisting in preaching morals: 'evitaba el ministerio del púlpito' (I, p.99). He much prefers research into biblical history. There is just a hint of paganism in his knowledge and love of ancient myths, and he is no biblical fundamentalist when it comes to considering the stories in the Old Testament, making his orthodoxy seem a trifle suspect to the literal-minded Don Jeromillo. His gentle scepticism and his mischievous sense of humour are revealed, too, in his accusation of dogmatic error over the abbess's confusion in the matter of the perfumed ointment poured over Jesus or of Doña Corazón's struggle to remember equally all three Persons of the Trinity. Nor is he beyond recounting irreverent anecdotes, as witness his story of Mossen Orduña and the unclad statue of the Virgin. He wears his priestly garb lightly, as he himself admits to Lóriz, and sees no virtue in constant self-denial and the abjuration of all worldly pleasures: 'desdeñaba a los obstinados en un género de virtud andrajosa y sudada como la del Padre Bellod' (I, p.94). His idea of virtue appears to be not so much God-centred as man-centred. To live quietly in a state of grace, of inner peace and contentment, he says, is to live at God's expense, and we should live at our own expense. Miró prefers not to expound upon this cryptic observation of Don Magín's, but its import will become clear much later in the story. Don Magín does not aspire to perfection or to unnecessary sacrifices: for him life itself is one long sacrifice. Towards the end of *El obispo leproso* we learn his secret: not that he has sinned, as Oleza expected a man like him to do, but that he has harboured a secret temptation for many years. Don Magín is in love with Purita, but all that he can hope for is that his enthusiasm will wane with the onset of old age, yet not knowing all the while whether his priestly sacrifice has been worth it:

> Todo pasa. ¿Todo? Pero ¿qué es lo que única y preci-
> samente pasará sino lo que fuimos, lo que hubiéramos
> gozado y alcanzado? Y si no pudimos ser ni saciar lo
> apetecido entonces ¿qué es lo que habrá pasado? ¿No

habrá pasado la posibilidad desaprovechada, la capaci-
dad recluida? ¿Y nuestro dolor? También nuestro dolor.
¿Y no quedará de algún modo lo que no fuimos ni
pudimos, y habremos pasado nosotros sin pasar?
Dolorosa consolación la de tener que decir: ¡Todo pasa,
si morimos con la duda de que no haya pasado todo: la
pasión no cumplida, la afición mortificada! (II, p.381)

The final scene of the novel is also the most poignant. Not cloyingly
sentimental — how could it be, set in the middle of a crowded
railway station full of street vendors calling out their wares and
their prices? — it succeeds in focusing on the inner tragedy of Don
Magín and bringing the story to a close on a deeply moving note.
The priest and Doña Purita, the two most cheerful characters in the
book, who have a capacity to enjoy life in the midst of a society
obsessed with sin, two characters seemingly made for each other,
but who choose to remain chaste, have to give up their pure friendship. Don Magín will not even have to continue enduring the
temptation of Purita's enticing presence. With his friend, protector,
and fellow-scholar, the Bishop, dead, with Purita gone, Don Magín
remains a lonely, forlorn figure. It is no doubt an irony intended by
Miró, and a cruel one, that a man who has been moved by a
generous concern for others should suffer the fate he has to suffer.
He has just persuaded himself that he must endure the continuing
sacrifice of not enjoying Doña Purita's sexual charms, when he
discovers that he is not even going to retain the consoling presence
of her personality. Such is Miró's insistence on the theme of happiness promised yet never fulfilled.

If it is not difficult to guess that Miró had a soft spot for the
unconventional Don Magín, then one might expect a similar
authorial affinity with the Bishop, true friend and kindred spirit. Yet
what is most striking about Miró's characterization of the Bishop is
its objectivity. The narrator seldom tells us what he is like; we are
simply shown him in various situations and invited to infer the
qualities of his personality. The major inference has to be that the
Bishop sees through the outward religion of the leading lights of

Oleza and does not like what he sees. He does not preach against false religious values, but at the same time he clearly does not wish to associate with their purveyors. The appointment of Bishop Céspedes was, for Don Amancio and his clerical coterie, a defeat. Despite their lobbying in favour of Don Cruz's appointment to the vacant see they had had an outsider imposed upon them, and Don Amancio will never forget this. The Bishop for his part remains an outsider, aloof from the petty attitudes and sanctimoniousness of respectable society in Oleza, and in turn unappreciated and unloved by most of its members. Upon his arrival the new prelate immediately breaks with tradition by not going directly to the church of San Daniel. He also prefers the company of Don Magín, regarded by the prim and proper of Oleza as an undisciplined priest, to the company of Don Cruz and his friends. He listens politely to the ladies' associations that come to visit him but he has little to say to them. Clearly he finds these visits entirely unnecessary and does not adhere to previous protocol. Similarly he accepts the offerings of relics and holy objects in good grace but evinces no faith in their power to effect miraculous cures. What impresses the Bishop are simple acts of charity, like Paulina's pleading on behalf of El Abuelo or Don Magín's generosity towards that same character. He himself always shows a deep concern for others, particularly those who are in some way disadvantaged. During the flood he insists on going out on foot to visit the parts of the town most in need of help. For the Holy Week processions he prefers to offer the balconies of his palace to the children from the hospice instead of to the privileged pupils of the Jesuit school. He consoles Don Daniel on his deathbed and urges that his daughter be brought to the side of the ailing father. Through the good offices of Don Magín he provides employment for Cara-rajada. Despite the hostility shown to him by the Jesuits he allows them to retain their premises and their school through the intercession of the most self-effacing of their members, the humble Father Ferrando. With Pablo he displays gentleness and understanding, both when he lets the seven-year-old play in his private chambers and when ten years later he confers upon the anxious adolescent the spiritual reassurance which he

craves. His interest is by no means limited to the spiritual welfare of
his flock. He is instrumental in bringing the railway to Oleza, he
helps the poorer parishes in his diocese, he pays for flood-protection
schemes, and he supports the establishment of a new social club. In
all this Miró has drawn a character of admirable qualities, but what
gives the personage the crucial and altogether fascinating dimension
is the horrible disease which he has to endure.

Neither the title of Volume II nor the gossip of the *olecenses*
about their bishop's disease proves that he is suffering from leprosy,
and the narrator never states that he is. But a comparison of the
description in the novel with the description of the clinical features
of the disease in medical texts leaves no doubt that Miró did intend
his character to be a leper. Indeed for a layman Miró has given an
impressively accurate, though incomplete, account of the symptoms
and course of the disease. The clinical symptoms are twice described
— first by the local doctor, Don Vicente Grifol, and later by the
more scientifically-minded foreign doctor — as external
manifestations of a hidden disease, which is none other than
infection of the body by the lepra bacillus. The incubation period of
the disease is of many years' duration, with dermal symptoms
manifesting themselves over a period of time. By the time of Don
Vicente Grifol's diagnosis the Bishop is forced to admit that his is a
long-standing illness which he has previously neglected. We can
observe the Bishop's natural anxiety as the external manifestations
become increasingly obvious, and his fear that he is suffering not
simply from a mere skin disorder but from a hideous and incurable
disease. The swelling of the fingers, the appearance of
hypopigmented macules which may darken as the disease
progresses, and the spreading of lesions to other parts of the body
such as knees and shoulders, are all symptoms correctly identified
by Miró. The chronic nature of the disease, with periods of
remission and relapse and with episodes of acute inflammation
known as reactions, is another feature that Miró accurately
documents in the Bishop's illness. But more interesting are certain
implied references to aspects of the disease which are less obvious.
At one point, for example, during a period of withdrawal, the

Bishop is heard to moan with pain and is seen to pierce his blisters with an implement sterilized over a flame. In lepromatous leprosy half the victims suffer from periods of reaction which result in the rapid appearance of painful papules or nodules in which the concentration of bacilli is highest and which may develop into ulcers, episodes which are accompanied by general malaise and pain and lead to prostration and weakness. And indeed the Bishop, after one of his relapses, reappears momentarily outside his chambers leaning on Don Magín and Pablo, 'con un cansancio y delgadez de convaleciente' (II, p.314). Finally, and revealingly from the perspective of Miró's knowledge of the disease, lepromatous leprosy can result in laryngitis, with hoarseness or stridor in the voice, and before the advent of modern medicine sufferers could die of laryngeal obstruction. In his penultimate appearance the Bishop's voice is said to be 'más afligida', and in his last appearance, having suffered a very sudden relapse, he tries in vain to speak as he sees Paulina in the doorway: 'el llagado hablaba saliéndole un soplo de su laringe podrida. Nadie le entendió' (II, p.362). A short while later the Bishop is dead. While avoiding describing the disease in clinical terminology, Miró has managed to give an account that remains remarkably faithful to real leprosy.[11]

Beyond the clinical symptoms of the disease one needs to ask whether Miró attaches any symbolic significance to the Bishop's leprosy. According to the abbess of La Visitación, the Bishop is popularly said to suffer for the sins of Oleza, an idea later repeated: 'El Señor le había elegido para salvar a Oleza. Y Oleza se cansaba de decirlo y oírlo' (II, p.350). There is, however, nothing to confirm that Miró, or for that matter the Bishop himself, shares the view of the Olezans. The Bishop does not appear to redeem anyone. And indeed a part of Oleza at least does not feel it needs redemption: '¿Ni redimir a estas horas de qué? Los hombres rubios pecadores, los extranjeros del ferrocarril, ya no estaban; y para los pecados del

---

[11]My medical information on leprosy is derived from *The Oxford Textbook of Medicine*, ed. Weatherall, Ledingham and Warrell, 2nd ed. (London: O.U.P., 1987), I, Section 5, pp.305–13.

lugar no era menester una víctima propiciatoria' (II, p.350). The Bishop's death does not change Oleza. What change there is, is material, not moral. The Bishop's leprosy is unlikely to have been intended by Miró himself as a symbol of Oleza's moral corruption; there is nothing to suggest that Oleza is any more corrupt than any other provincial town or that any immorality it harbours comes to an end with the Bishop's death. What there is, however, as Ricardo Gullón has pointed out (9, p.28), is a contrastive parallelism between the Bishop's leprosy, real but blameless, and the leprosy that afflicts Oleza, metaphorical but guilt-ridden. Indeed Oleza is referred to by the narrator as 'un cuerpo llagado' (II, p.168).

But if Miró discourages us from seeing in the Bishop's suffering Oleza's redemption, there is no doubt that the Bishop is characterized in such a way as to bring Christ to mind. To suggest that he is a Christ-symbol might be to press the parallel too far, since Miró tends to make a stylistic habit out of biblical allusion. Yet the Bishop's acceptance of his own suffering, his concern for the suffering of others, his empathy with children, his gentleness and exhortation to love rather than commination, are all qualities that make him a Christ-like figure. At the same time there is a deliberate reversal of the traditional association of leprosy with impurity and sin (17, p.66), an association originating in the Old Testament and persisting even beyond Hansen's discovery of the lepra bacillus in 1873. On more than one occasion the leprous Bishop is described as being pure, and the contrast between his decaying body and his pure soul is explicitly made: 'la carne padecida, carne del hombre puro que le miraba' (II, p.353). The Bishop is associated with the lemon tree, the fruit of which has cleansing properties and which, as was seen earlier, is used as a symbol of purity. Moreover his behaviour is morally impeccable, despite the accusations levelled against him by the puritans of Oleza. That a man without a stain on his character should be struck down by a disease which blemishes his body is no doubt a tragic irony, but Miró does not in fact suggest that Oleza shuns its bishop because he is a leper. If the Bishop becomes a recluse it is because he chooses to be so. He is clearly very conscious of his disfigurement, hence his constant wearing of gloves and scarf.

On one occasion, as he sits underneath his favourite lemon tree, he reaches up to rub off the perfume of its young leaves onto his hands: 'y las vio llagadas y no quiso tocar la hermosura del árbol' (II, p.353). The Bishop's leprosy, then, would appear to be not something that he has to suffer for others but something that he has to suffer by himself. He chooses to suffer in silence and shares his suffering with no-one: 'se quedaba a solas con su dolor' (II, p.163). In his presence nobody refers to his disease, not even his closest companion, Don Magín. The Bishop seeks no sympathy, no pity, no consolation. What Miró has emphasized above all is the reality and the loneliness of his suffering. In this respect he is but a more vivid, remarkable, and moving example of the adversity that befalls so many of the characters in their ordinary lives. Like the Bishop's leprosy, adversity is part and parcel of the human situation, Miró appears to be saying; it has no explanation and no cure.

5. Minor Characters. Oleza as Protagonist

In addition to the fifteen characters considered in the preceding chapters there are some thirty others with significant personalities, some of whose roles are scarcely less important than those of the major personages already studied. Such is the case, for example, of Don Vicente Grifol, the elderly doctor who looks after Don Daniel, Don Magín, and the Bishop, characterized by Don Magín as 'el viejecito más puro' of Oleza (II, p.147). Frustrated in his love for Doña Corazón, he remains a kindly and courageous figure, ignored by Oleza yet clearly enjoying the sympathy of his creator.[12] He is a man of independent mind, who cares not what the respectable society of Oleza thinks of him, and who gently but firmly dismisses the Bishop's biblical self-diagnosis. Though absent-minded in his old age, he is full of memories of a distant time. He has the capacity to recall very particular details of past events, and this is one of his two major functions within the novel, to act as observer of past and present: the other, not unconnected with his reminiscences, is to underline the theme of the might-have-been, a vision of life as consisting of parallel possibilities of which only one can be experienced and the others merely imagined nostalgically.

The other local doctor, Monera the homeopath, is a deliberate contrast to Don Vicente. Whereas the latter is self-assured, well-bred and independent, Monera is ill at ease, socially graceless, and toadyish. He is a social climber who throws in his lot with the ultra-conservative Carlist high society for the sake of social status, and his humble origins are betrayed by his awkward manner and his sense of inferiority. Though he is professionally successful, his social pretensions turn him into a pathetic figure as he suffers the

---

[12]Perhaps more than just his sympathy. Marian Coope argues that Don Vicente embodies Miró's novelistic theory (7).

barely disguised contempt of his adopted social companions, Don Cruz, Father Bellod and Don Amancio, and the hysterical outbursts of his childless wife. Miró treats him as something of a fun figure, not least in his nervous mannerism — taking out his large gold watch at moments of discomfiture — and his characterization adds a good deal of ironic humour to the novel.

The secondary characters of the Oleza novels cover the whole social gamut, from the titled aristocracy represented by the Condes de Lóriz to the lowly inhabitants of the San Ginés slums represented by La Amortajadora. The role of the Lóriz family is important: it forms a counterpoint to the Galindo family (*24*, p.80). The Galindos are the leading Carlist family of Oleza, while the Lórizs belong to the Liberal establishment and are well connected in government circles in the capital, since they are able to help the Bishop in his attempt to bring the railway to Oleza. The Count and Countess are polished, self-assured and full of easy charm, conscious that their position enables them to befriend the urbane Don Magín as well as to entertain the forbidding Jesuits and their charges. The atmosphere in their home is relaxed and welcoming, the presence of the Countess's cousins adding an air of joviality that contrasts with the conventional gravity of the Holy Week solemnities. The Countess is portrayed as beautiful, intelligent, and engaging, the Count as suave and subtly decadent, the son as unruly and old-looking, Máximo, the Countess's brother, as romantic and seductive, her cousins as full of life. The women in particular are singled out for their radiance and lack of affectation: 'Apareció la familia de Lóriz. La condesa y sus primas forasteras. Dejaban claridad, gracia, frescor y aroma de frutales finos en flor. Luz y goce de naturaleza' (II, p.206). Nowhere does Miró suggest that the Lórizs are a model family, but, for all their aristocratic style, they are shown to lead a more natural life than the Galindos and to entertain an altogether more modern outlook.

More modern, too, but in this case caricatures of modernity, are María Fulgencia's uncle and his newly-acquired French wife, Ivette/Kate/Gothon/ Ivonne-Catherine, described as the product of a fashion designer. María Fulgencia's cousin, Mauricio, the Hussar

captain and military attaché at the Vienna embassy, also comes
close to being a caricature, not least because he is in part seen
through the eyes of the nuns, who regard him as a heavenly
messenger or archangel: 'Capitán y diplomático, con él habían
entrado en La Visitación las milicias y las cancillerías de casi toda
Europa. Y la abadesa y sus hijas le miraban, pareciéndoles recién
venido de la Jerusalén celeste' (II, p.233). Mauricio's military
comportment sits ill at ease both with the social and religious
etiquette of the convent and with the educated simplicity of the
Bishop's chambers, and Miró uses the occasion to offer a gentle
satire of military pomposity. The Dean, too, is semi-caricature, his
utter inability to make any kind of decision or cope with any new
situation being rationalized by his maxim that 'las cosas son según
son' (I, p.82). It is fairly obvious that the Dean has above all a
structural function. In Volume I his role is reduced to a couple of
pages and the odd passing reference: we know him first as the uncle
of Doña Corazón's suitor and eventual husband, and then as the
acting bishop pending the appointment of a new pastor to the vacant
see. His real function is seen in Volume II, where he is the means of
introducing the María Fulgencia complication into the novel.
Despite the essentially functional nature of his role Miró has drawn
his character with a fine sense of humour. A kindly and well-
meaning person, he is utterly impractical and quite incapable of
dealing with his protégée. When told that María Fulgencia wishes to
buy the famous statue of the Angel de Salcillo all he can think of is
where on earth she might find a fitting place for it. María
Fulgencia's tantrums, eccentricities, and instabilities totally baffle
the poor man, and he gives in to her whims at every turn in the
belief that he has at last found the solution to the problem and can
safely return to the calm of his beloved calligraphy.

   The coterie of Carlist women, of whom Elvira is the leading
light and La Monera the arriviste, is completed with Las Catalanas.
Their major function is to act as audience for Elvira's scandalous
tales of licentiousness and depravity, but Miró has drawn them to
perfection in all their nullity. They are almost complete nonentities,
with nothing to do, nothing to say and virtually nothing to think.

Their characterization rests precisely upon their lack of individuality, since the novelist does not even distinguish between the two
sisters, not even when one of them dies: ' una de las *catalanas* — la
mayor o la menor — había muerto' (II, p.380). They do not even
appear to change: everyone remembers them as ever having been as
they are now. Their lives are monotonous, predictable, and colour-
less. Credulous, simple-minded, and inexperienced, they prefer to
believe Elvira's lies about other people's sexual behaviour rather
than accept the possibility of calumny. Las Catalanas represent
provincial uselessness, but unlike Elvira they are comparatively
innocent and harmless.

The members of Don Amancio's household are neither
innocent nor harmless. The master may be sexually abstemious, but
the rest of the inhabitants of his house are only too ready to indulge
in sexual horseplay of the crudest kind. Diego *el giboso* is deformed
not merely physically but morally too, while Tonda is simply brutal.
The compliant female servants are barely drawn, something which,
curiously, is true of the work as a whole: domestic servants are
ignored by Miró, with the exception of Jimena, whom he has
characterized at some length despite her limited role. As Don
Daniel's housekeeper, Jimena is no ordinary servant; indeed to
Paulina she is more like a mother than a maidservant, and she is not
afraid to contradict her master over the suitability of Don Alvaro as
a husband for Paulina, seeing in him an 'hombre de altar y no de
amorío', as she puts it (I, p.124), for, like the statue of Nuestro
Padre, with whom she compares him, he lacks warmth and tenderness. Fiercely protective towards Paulina, she has forebodings on
the day of the wedding and prays that she will be brave enough to
call to account those responsible for Paulina's happiness if it were
not fulfilled. Of course Jimena's brave intentions come to nothing
once Paulina falls into the clutches of Alvaro and Elvira, as Don
Magín rather pointedly reminds her. But unlike Doña Corazón she
is not overawed by Doña Elvira or her brother, and furiously
confronts them in their own house to demand Paulina's presence at
her father's bedside. With the disappearance of Don Daniel,
Jimena's role is effectively over, but it is perhaps some indication of

Miró's own valuation of the character that he considers it worth-while bringing her into the story briefly at the end of Volume I and again in Volume II in the guise of Doña Corazón's nurse and companion. Loyal, courageous, and down-to-earth, Jimena represents the qualities of humble provincial folk at their best.

No less interesting a figure despite her more fleeting appearances is Doña Nieves *la santera*. Imperturbable and inexpressive, this enigmatic character is said by Don Magín to have unrivalled knowledge of Oleza's secrets, achieved through the access which her trade gives her to Oleza's homes, an accomplishment confirmed by the narrator: 'su altarillo era su refugio, su alacena, su escudo y su llave para llegar a lo recóndito de todos los corazones y viviendas' (II, p. 181). Despite the complete absence of any perceivable trace of emotion, as her name implies, she is not averse to providing her services as layer-out free of charge, choosing instead to live from the alms that her porterage of the image of St Joseph brings. Oleza says of her that she sleeps nightly in the death robes of a nun, but Doña Nieves remains silent, like her San Josefico, listening and observing. In her case religion is a means not of manipulation, as it is in the case of Don Cruz and the Jesuits, but simply of penetrating the veneer of propriety of the socially important people of the town. Doña Nieves is the ears and eyes of Oleza, on good terms with all the principal families irrespective of ideological alignment, but she is no gossip-monger or detractor. She simply knows, but makes no accusation. Thus, when she takes the little altar-piece with its image to the Galindos' house she casually mentions to Paulina that San Josefico has just spent the night in Máximo's bedroom, where the Countess's brother had insisted on placing it on hearing of its destination on the morrow, upon learning which, Paulina does not dare to look into San Josefico's eyes: 'Paulina no pudo mirarlo. Los ojos infantiles de San Josefico eran más pavorosos que los ojos adivinos de Nuestro Padre San Daniel; y la llamaban como si quisieran que recogiese una culpable intimidad. San Josefico se parecía esa noche a doña Nieves...' (II, p.229). And Doña Nieves it is who is chosen by Miró as a witness to the final encounter and parting of Don Magín and Doña Purita, as if she had shared their secret all along.

Rather less intriguing as a character is Cara-rajada's mother, La Amortajadora, although her history is not without interest. Thrust into penurious widowhood after a comfortable existence by her own son's misplaced generosity and enthusiasm for the Carlist uprising, she is reduced to laying out corpses and haunting the churches of Oleza to plead among the statues and the churchgoers for aid for her epileptic son. A mixture of motherly grief, religious superstition and anger at her son's abandonment ('le han desamparado todos', she complains: I, p.147), she is certainly a pitiful figure and another victim of misplaced ideological zeal, but one whose relevance to the story is only marginal. With Cara-rajada dead, Miró has no suitable role for La Amortajadora and replaces her in Volume II with the better integrated figure of Doña Nieves.

The gallery of clerics is widened further by the mention of a considerable number of men of the cloth given minor but specific roles. Mossen Orduña, for example, the archivist at the episcopal palace, is amusingly characterized as an unworldly, absent-minded archaeologist, oblivious of what goes on around him and living in a time-scale different from that of his fellow citizens, yet who in public is anxious to mask the tremor of a limb. His appearance is once again limited to Volume I; by Volume II he has died after completing his life's work on Marian iconography and furnishing Don Magín with an amusing anecdote. The *capellán Abuelo* merits the odd passing mention. He is merely characterized by old age and lack of means, his essential function being to show Don Magín's generosity and resourcefulness in offering him a home. He is another of the characters who do not survive into Volume II. Monsignor Salom, the Jesuits' guest at the prizegiving and end-of-year celebration, is another variation on priestly unworldliness. He is no scholar, however, and appears nonplussed by the pretentious name-dropping and erudite conversation of his hosts. Although no more than an obscure prelate from the Middle East, he is perceived by Oleza as a saint and martyr because of his mutilated hand, a self-inflicted wound the cause of which sends the sensitive women of Oleza into raptures. Despite Miró's undoubtedly ironic presentation of this particular kind of penance, Monsignor Salom is portrayed not unsympathetically, particularly in comparison with the Jesuits milling around him. He is a man of simple tastes and modest expression, completely lacking in the subtleties and hypocrisy of those who use his presence to impress the local population and thereby enhance their standing. The world of Oleza, with its obsessive preoccupation with sensuality and sin, is alien to this missionary bishop from distant lands who longs to return to 'la obscuridad de su vicariato' (II, p.271).

By contrast, the Jesuits aspire to anything but obscurity. The way in which they insinuate themselves among the local population by shrewd public relations until they exercise a dominant influence is brilliantly portrayed by Miró through brief descriptive touches (for example, they go to the trouble of being seen to pray in the parish church of the patron saint of Oleza). The Jesuits of Oleza possess not just a school but an empire: 'El colegio se infundía en toda la ciudad. La ciudad equivalía a un patio de "Jesús", un patio sin clausura, y los Padres y Hermanos lo cruzaban como si no saliesen de su casa' (II, p.106). The moral vigilance exerted by the Jesuits over Oleza, above all through their influence upon the female population, produces boredom and apathy. The only spectacles allowed are those authorized by the Society of Jesus. When a group of local men, having observed the more pleasurable existence of the visiting railway workers, rebels against the drabness of life in Oleza and decides to enliven the local scene, Don Magín warns them that without the approval of the Society of Jesus the scheme will fail, upon hearing which their courage begins to wilt: 'Todos ellos encontrarían en su mujer, en sus hermanas, en su madre, en su novia, una voluntad encogida, necesitada siempre de la consulta y legitimación de otras voluntades' (II, p.160). This urge of the Jesuits to set themselves up as Oleza's guardian angels, as Miró labels them, is accompanied by the Society's preoccupation with its privileged social position. They feel pride and self-satisfaction at having brought the Bishop of Aleppo to officiate at the Corpus Christi festivities and the prize-giving ceremony at their school; but Miró allows the reader to appreciate, through the soliloquy of another character, that it is not the person of Monsignor Salom that interests the Jesuits, for once his public mission is assured, the Jesuits cease to concern themselves with the welfare of their penurious guest: '[...] y los RR. PP. de "Jesús", que tan afanosamente le buscaron, ya no se cuidaban sino de sus solemnidades y vacaciones' (II, p.262). On another occasion the Corpus Christi sermon is delivered by a Jesuit. Mannered, bombastic, and overflowing with theological learning, its intended theatrical effect is frustrated by the taste for simplicity of the Bishop of Oleza who, no sooner has the Jesuit come to the end of his oration, and without even giving him time to descend from the pulpit, completely undercuts the preacher by addressing the faithful himself, 'claro, dulce y lento', while the Jesuit, deprived of his oratorical triumph, is obliged to listen motionless, 'con el bonete en el pecho y un dardo en cada cristal de sus gafas' (II, p.161). The theological presumptuousness and intellectual snobbishness of the Jesuits, the belief that their interpretation of the liturgy is better than that of any other church in the diocese, their display of useless erudition, pedantry, and false intellectual values (for them true science lies in handling first editions and obscure treatises), are all aspects of Miró's satirical portrayal, a satire that is all the more effective for the complete absence of invective or condemnation. Indeed Miró's approach is based above all on irony, of which there are touches of amusing ingenuity. When, relaxing in the garden after prize-giving, Monsignor Salom grants permission to smoke, the kill-joy Jesuits receive this concession ungraciously. The Capuchin Franciscan Father Agullent recalls how, running out of tobacco in the Sinai, he himself sought out and dried substitute grasses for his pipe, whereupon the Jesuit Father Neira attempts to devalue Father Agullent's anecdote and discredit the storyteller, only to fall victim to Miró's exquisite irony:

> El P. Neira odiaba esas sensuales memorias, y
> murmuró con voz muy delgada:
> -Repare, monseñor, en el P. Francisco de Agullent:
> tiene la barba roja, como Judas.

> El capuchino tocó suavemente sus vellones bermejos,
> y dijo con simplicidad:
>
> —¿De veras, de veras que resulta comprobado que
> Judas fuese rojo? ¡Quién sabe, Dios mío! No hallé
> ningún texto que lo afirme. Ni si era flaco, ni menudo,
> ni oriondo: ¡nada! ¡Lo único cierto es que Judas
> perteneció a la compañía de Jesús! (II, p.270)

The Jesuits' claim to superiority, their self-sufficiency, their
subordination of all interests to those of the Society, and the manipulation of other people for their own ends, are all aspects subtly but
unequivocally brought out by Miró in his portrayal. Thus, for
example, we can observe how the Padre Rector, so solicitous
towards Don Alvaro when he believes the survival of the Jesuit
school to depend on the Society being able to lay its hands on El
Olivar, undergoes a complete change of attitude, making Don
Alvaro wait and insinuating a lack of true spirit of sacrifice on his
part, once it is clear that the survival of the school is not dependent
on the Egea estate. The Jesuits' aspiration to perfection is seen by
Miró — although he never says so directly — as pretentious and
inhuman, an aspiration which reveals pride rather than the humility
they pretend to personify with their clasped hands and lowered eyes.
The contrast with Don Magín's personal philosophy cannot be
greater. Miró's portrayal of the Jesuits, though amusing because of
its pointed irony, is deeply critical. They may not stand out as
individuals, but their collective values and behaviour are unmistak-
ably portrayed and quietly denounced. The one significant exception
among the dozen or so identified by name or office is the most
humble and most ignored member of the Society, Father Ferrando,
who spends his life visiting the poor to offer them salvation. And, in
a typical Mironian inversion of values, the lowliest priest it is who is
called upon to act as confessor to the highest.

The laity employed at the Colegio de Jesús is represented by
Señor Hugo, the Swedish gym master, and Don Roger, the music
teacher and bass singer. They are to a degree caricatures: one small,
round, and sweet-looking, the other tall, athletic, and vain, but both

equally deficient at their profession, and, what is worse, submissive and compliant to the ferocious discipline of their employers, who demand, as the price of re-employment in 'Jesús', that they end their friendship with the lovely Doña Purita.

The picture of clerical society in Oleza would not be complete without some reference to female members of the clergy. Some half-a-dozen orders of nuns are listed as having houses in Oleza, but only one, the *salesas* or Order of the Visitation, is portrayed (with a good deal of allusion to the co-founders of the order, St Francis de Sales and St Jane Frances Frémyot, and to its early history). Also mentioned is the Order of the Little Sisters of the Poor, in the context of the Maundy Thursday collection. Since women in holy orders have traditionally played a much less prominent role than male members of the clergy, Miró needed some device that would allow him to bring them into the picture without it seeming an irrelevant intrusion. He has done so most adroitly, primarily by using María Fulgencia as the connecting link between the nuns and the mainstream characters, and secondarily by making Don Jeromillo chaplain of the convent of La Visitación, thereby facilitating reference to the other inhabitants of the convent. Miró's portrayal of the nuns has a hint of satirical humour about it but it is by no means as critical as his portrayal of the Jesuits. The nuns' attachment to their furniture is amusing in a community given to the pursuit of spiritual values. They provide seating for the many visitors to Don Jeromillo's quarters during Don Magín's convalescence, but they lend the chairs one at a time, with pained reluctance, counting them out and counting them in again each evening. They have a touching faith in the miraculous powers of the relic of the foundress and are deeply concerned that recalling the relic from the Bishop's palace might forestall a miraculous cure. Unused to the world, they are easily dazzled by the magnificent uniform of the young Hussar and show an eager curiosity which the locutory grill cannot hide. The young nuns are portrayed as impressionable adolescents susceptible of romantic flights of fancy. Of the older nuns two are individually characterized. The abbess is kindly, tolerant, somewhat indecisive, and fearful of the complications created by María Fulgencia's unstable character. The *Clavaria* by contrast is a fierce disciplinarian, inquisitorial, intolerant, and resentful of Maria Fulgencia's intrusion, a resentment which leads to the petty execution of one of the latter's turtle doves. The convent of La Visitación does not quite live up to the 'quietud de dulzura mariana' (I, p.65) mentioned at the start of the work (and indeed the objective of the foundress). Here, too, human passions, and the concomitant attempt to suppress them, are seen to be at work, though perhaps in their more comic dimension.

The staff at the episcopal palace is often mentioned, usually in the context of visitors who arrive or depart, but Miró's treatment eschews individual portrayal, with the exception of Mossen Orduña (we do get a good impression, nevertheless, of the iciness, impassivity and stonewalling of the secretary who has to keep importunate visitors at bay). Life in the palace is shown to be busy, and not simply because of the constant stream of visitors and messengers but because there is a hum of activity amongst the palace staff, not least in the gardens, where young Pablo comes to play amidst the dogs, the geese and the doves, an atmosphere altogether different from the sepulchral echoes of the church of Nuestro Padre. The motto on the entrance of the palace, *Pulsate et aperietur vobis* (taken from St Matthew 7:7) is no empty legend; the Bishop's residence is a welcoming place, but the reaction to it is not uniformly positive. Don Magín, Pablo, even Don Vicente Grifol, take to the palace unreservedly, and in their presence the words *sol, luminosidad, claridad* are used to describe its appearance, as if these were qualities conferred by the observer rather than intrinsic to the object itself. On the other hand Don Amancio and Father Bellod find no gladness, no solace, in the Bishop's palace: for them it is but a symbol of indifference.

At the bottom of the social heap are the *arrabaleros* of San Ginés, whose very superfluity from the narrow perspective of the plot tells us something of Miró's approach to his novel. He has chosen to complete the social picture of Oleza by including a description of the slums of San Ginés and their inhabitants, though what is clearly important in Miró's scheme of things is the attitude

of other social groupings or individuals to the socially disadvantaged. San Ginés is not there to complete merely the geography of
the place but rather its ideological characterization. What character-
izes San Ginés in the immediate sense is poverty, filth, and disease.
Miró does not eschew description of the sordidness of the place or of
the roughness of the inhabitants: 'arrabal de astrosos, bravos y
descreídos' (I, p.145). Yet amidst the deprivation there is neither
hatred nor despair, except in the extreme case of Cara-rajada. The
Carlists of the Círculo de Labradores may feel themselves threat-
ened by the slum-dwellers of San Ginés on the eve of San Daniel,
but the threat exists in their own closed minds only, for the slum-
dwellers refuse to heed Cara-rajada's incitement. Ignored by the
rich of Oleza the *arrabaleros* may be, but there is no alienation on
their part; they feel themselves to be as much a part of Oleza as
those who live in the wealthier quarters: '¡De los de abajo y de
nosotros es lo mesmo Nuestro Padre San Daniel!' (I, p.255). They
may not go to church, but they maintain good relations with Don
Magín and call upon his services in their final moments. Nor are
they without pity and generosity, for they offer the repulsive Cara-
rajada their 'compasión y amistad' (I, p.254) as well as food. Yet
this generosity turns to cruelty when Cara-rajada, having abandoned
San Ginés to become a *señoritingo*, tries to enlist them for his own
purposes. The *arrabaleros*, too, have their pride and will not take
insults from a turncoat.

But beyond individual and social groups lies the city of Oleza
itself, 'el gran personaje de la novela [...] que [...] se constituye en
el factor dominante que envuelve y devora a sus propios hijos' (*30*,
p.33). The portrait of Oleza is built up piecemeal, description of a
street here, of a church or convent there, mention of the river, of a
bridge, of orchards and their fragrances. The only description of the
city in its entirety is the view from the departing train which is
carrying Purita to a new life. Yet in an important sense Oleza is
characterized not by physical descriptions but rather by what goes
on within its walls. Miró places considerable emphasis on the
religious and social activities — which often come down to the
same thing — of particular groups. These descriptions, however,

whether of Holy Week processions, Corpus Christi festivities, the feast of San Daniel, or the various social clubs, are not offered for the sake of *costumbrismo* or local colour. The accent is very much on what the activities betray of the mental outlook of the people.

To list all the various activities of the *olecenses* mentioned in the novel would be lengthy, but certain of them do stand out. The number of religious societies is enormous, and though some exist for quite specific purposes (e.g. Adoración Nocturna), others appear to have only vaguely charitable ends (e.g. the Juntas de Señoras) which Miró does not insist upon, or else are aimed at recruiting the youth of the town (e.g. Hijas de María, Congregación de San Luis). What he does insist upon is that any social organization in Oleza must be deemed to have a religious basis, and that purely secular organizations will be resisted at all costs by the influential and ultra-conservative clergy. The Círculo de Labradores — which, unlike many of the other societies mentioned, is fictitious — is the Carlist Club of Oleza, closely associated with the local landowning class and enjoying the support of the more traditionally-minded clergy. The bookcases of the somewhat decrepit Círculo are stocked with religious books. Rather less influential in Oleza, it would appear, than the Carlist Círculo is the Liberal Casino, which Miró scarcely dwells upon. The Nuevo Casino is an offshoot or modernized version of the older institution, set up with the intention of challenging Carlist supremacy by the installation of billiard tables. Yet even at this stage entertainment in Oleza is regulated by the ultra-conservative element: 'No había más pasatiempos que los aprobados por la comunidad de "Jesús" y por la comunidad del Penitenciario. Procesiones de Semana Santa; juntas de las cofradías; coloquios de señoras con señoras, de hombres con hombres; tertulias de archivos; comedias de Navidad en el *De Profundis* de "Jesús"' (II, p.158). Curiously, for a city under the control of a reactionary clergy that prides itself on its austerity, Oleza is said to have its own brothel, presumably outside the control of Canon Cruz and the Jesuits. It is the arrival of the railway workers, with their laxer habits and merrymaking, that arouses the envy of the timorous men of the Nuevo Casino and prompts them to propose the founding of the

Recreo Benéfico to provide unsegregated entertainment under the umbrella of a charitable organization, which prompts the shrewd Don Magín to exclaim sceptically: '¡Ah, vamos: la obra de caridad, la alcahueta de siempre!' (II, p.160). Yet with the support of Don Magín and the approval of the Bishop the Recreo Benéfico is established, to be denounced by *Alba Longa* in his newspaper as a source of perdition for the families of Oleza and anathematized by Father Bellod as a *gusanera*. The activities of the Recreo Benéfico are harmless enough, but they are presented by Miró as indicating some modest degree of emancipation of the inhabitants from the traditional arbiters of social life:

> Como en el mundo, las dos mitades de Oleza, la honesta
> y la relajada, se acometían para trastornar la conciencia
> y la apariencia de la vida. 'Jesús' esforzaba a los
> olecenses puros. Ya no se temía la discordia como un
> mal, sino que era un deber soltarla en lo íntimo de las
> amistades y de las familias. El Recreo Benéfico, con su
> mote masónico de caridad, iba pudriendo las limpias
> costumbres. Muñía bailes, jiras, cosos, tómbolas,
> comedias y verbenas, que 'Jesús' condenaba implacable,
> repudiando a los luises que participaban de las
> abominaciones. (II, p.304)

Although the narrative point of view in this passage is that of the clerical ultra-conservatives, it serves nevertheless to indicate that the Jesuits and their allies are beginning to lose their grip on Oleza. Just how much Oleza changes, Miró does not clearly state. If anything he underplays the change, especially from a moral or religious point of view. The Carlists may complain that Liberal influence undermines religion and good habits; but the truth is that Liberal dissidence is, from a religious point of view, much more apparent than real. Whether Liberals or Carlists, all Olezans are believers: 'En Oleza no había ni un enemigo de la fe [...]. Integros y liberales eran de la cofradía de "Jesús atado"' (II, p.170). And while the welcome given to the railway engineers — so much more attractive than the introverted men of the Juventud Católica — by some local families is deplored by the Carlist and Jesuit caucus, others recall that during the Carlist wars the arrival in town of the young horseriders of the faction was the signal for the young women of Oleza to climb on the horse's rump and regale the men with kisses. All that has changed therefore is the political allegiance of the newcomers: the interest of the local women in the menfolk who arrive from afar remains. Even though it is true that Miró is in part depicting a provincial world beginning to be eroded by the effects of new technology and new customs, it is all too easy to exaggerate the clash between the old and the new. For if the real clash were simply that between an old and a new conception of the world, why then have recourse to several of the older characters in the novel — Jimena the maidservant, Don Vicente Grifol, Doña Corazón — to embody those positive qualities of giving rather than forbidding that Miró uses to place clerical Oleza in such a bad light? The clash, if clash it is, is much more profound: it is that between those who hold a dogmatic view of life dominated by the concept of sin and the concomitant need to flee from every enjoyment, and those who live with arms open to those simple pleasures that life may offer us. Rather than change, then, Miró suggests the possibility of change. By the end of the novel, with the Carlist faction in terminal decline, with the railway bringing an increased commercial activity and a new prosperity to Oleza, with improvements in civic amenities, with little apparent interest in the fortunes of the vacant see, Oleza is at the dawn of a new age, even if the women from San Ginés still walk around ill-fed, unwashed, and unshod. But the Oleza of Miró's novel is not the Oleza of a Liberal, progressive, or emergent Spain. On the contrary, it is by and large a symbol of a retrograde and unenlightened Spain. I shall explore this further in the final chapter.

In chapter II we saw that it is possible to establish temporal reference points in this novel both in relation to external or historical time and in relation to internal or novelistic time. Miró's concern is not just with the past, however; that is to say, it is much more than that of a historian seeking to establish a true picture of the past. Miró's preoccupation, though difficult to describe with exactitude, appears to be with the nature of time itself; time seen not from a scientific vantage point but from a purely human one, a phenomenon not independent of man but hazily perceived during moments of heightened awareness. For this reason the exploration of the nature of time is almost invariably carried out through a character's consciousness. Memory has a good deal to do with it, but the theme of time in the Oleza novels is not confined to a simple process of recall, just as the coming of the railway means more than simply the destruction of the past. There is a strong presence of the past in this novel, perhaps because Miró himself brings his own past into the book as he writes, so that the intermingling of past and present moments acquires a particular function as it is transferred from author to character. It is highly significant that several of the major characters are made to recall, almost to re-live at times, events and scenes from their past. This is especially true of Volume II, although examples can also be found in Volume I. By memory in this sense, then, I do not mean simply a character telling another character of something that happened years before; I mean, rather, a process of spontaneous, even unconscious, recall in which a character is suddenly transported to an event or an experience that took place at some point in the past; something sets the process in motion, a sense impression, a chance thought. Nor is it simply a matter of an older person reminiscing, since young Pablo is also affected by this invasion of the present moment by the past. In the very first chapter of *El obispo leproso*, Pablo, during one of his visits to the episcopal palace in the company of Don Magín, meets the Bishop for the first time. The Bishop reminds him of the occasion when mother and son were walking past his residence in tears, and when they saw him looking down from his window he blessed them. The Bishop now asks the seven-year-old boy why they were crying; but Pablo cannot remember, he is too busy with his discoveries on the Bishop's desk. He settles down in the Bishop's chair to play with the various wondrous implements spread out upon the desk — a forbidden area at home — and gradually that sad afternoon invades his consciousness:

> Se distrajo con un pisapapeles de cristal, lleno de iris. Poco a poco la tarde recordada por el prelado se le acercó hasta tenerla encima de su frente, como los vidrios de sus balcones donde se apoyaba muchas veces, sin ver nada, volviéndose de espaldas al aburrimiento. Todo aquel día tocaron las campanas lentas y rotas. Tarde de las Animas, ciega de humo de río y de lluvia. La casa se rajó de gritos del padre. Ardían las luces de aceite delante de los cuadros de los abuelos — el señor Galindo, la señora Serrallonga — , que le miraban sin haberle visto y sin haberle amado nunca. Cuando el padre y tía Elvira se fueron, las campanas sonaron más grandes. Le buscó su madre; la vio más delgada, más blanca. Se ampararon los dos en ellos mismos, y entonces las luces eran las que los miraban, crujiendo tan viejas como si las hubiesen encendido los abuelos. Después, la madre y el hijo salieron por el postigo de los trascorrales. Todo el atardecer se quejaba con la voz del río. Caminaban entre árboles mojados rojos del otoño. Pablo agarróse a una punta del manto de la madre, prendido de llovizna como un rosal.
>
> Ella no pudo resistir su congoja, y cayó de rodillas. Una mano morada trazó la cruz entre la niebla, y ellos

la sintieron descender sobre sus frentes afligidas... (II, p.90)

This remembrance of the past is more than just an effort of memory on the part of Pablo. He has moved back in time and is hearing the bells and the angry shouts of his father, perceiving the rain and the mist and his mother's distress at his own anguish. Much later the same scene is recalled by Paulina as she lies half-asleep with Pablo next to her. Mother and son have just been reunited after she had been prevented, through the jealousy of her husband and sister-in-law, from going to fetch Pablo at the end of the school year and attending the prize-giving ceremony for the school-leavers. Pablo's anger is gradually attenuated by his mother's comforting presence:

> Paulina le abrazó. La madre y el hijo se fueron quedando dormidos bajo la evocación de aquellos años, en una quietud profunda y clara como una bóveda de firmamento; y la tarde de junio los envolvía de suavidad; la tarde, allí tan parada encima de la vega, tenía la pureza y la fragilidad de un vidrio sagrado, y, a veces, se rompía de aleteos de campanas y músicas del Corpus. Y en la tarde tan ancha se traslucía otra tarde muy remota, ciega de nieblas que iban creciendo del río. Campanas de Todos los Santos. Paulina y su hijo caminaban abriendo el humo de la lluvia; y al pasar por el huerto de palacio se arrodillaron para recibir la piedad de una mano que los bendecía y de unos ojos tristes que los acompañaron desde lejos. (II, p.280)

That dreadful afternoon many years ago lies buried in Paulina's subconscious; what is it that sparks off the process of recall as she lies half-asleep with her son beside her? Miró does not tell us; instead we read:

> De pronto, Paulina se revolvió sobresaltada, y sus latidos le resonaron en todo el dormitorio. Venía la voz

del esposo:

—¡Pablo, Pablo!

El hijo se le apretó más, mirando a lo profundo de la casa, ya obscura.

—¡Pablo! (II, p.281)

The common element in the present scene and the past scene is the angry shouts of Don Alvaro. In her state of semi-consciousness Paulina hears the threatening shouts of her husband and her mind momentarily takes her back to that other afternoon when mother and son had ventured out into the streets following the angry ravings of Don Alvaro and had been consoled by the look of understanding and the blessing of a generous spirit. The original event itself has no separate existence in the narrative: it exists only in the minds of the Bishop, Paulina, and Pablo. What is important, therefore, is not so much the event in itself, when it happened, as the fact that it is being recalled now, that it is a part of the psychological make-up of these three characters. Perhaps what Miró is saying is that memory tells us as much about the present as about the past.

Memories of childhood often affect both Paulina and Pablo. While Paulina frequently remembers her happy, carefree days at El Olivar, Pablo recalls his happy days in the Bishop's palace when, sent by his mother on a mission to save El Olivar, he wanders in again after an absence of many years. His old friend Ranca, who used to look after the orchard and carry him on his shoulders to the Bishop's quarters, is dead:

¡Ranca había muerto, y el huerto se quedaba! [...]. Le dio la terciana y se murió y el huerto seguía [...]. ¡Tanto tiempo estaba ya el hortal en ese abandono, que hasta pasó la muerte muy callando entre los árboles! Pablo sintió el vuelo de los años encima de su corazón. Y todo lo que se quedó coordinado y dormido en su primera infancia le resalía ahora con sensación de presencia. (II, p.309)

What Miró is underlining is not simply the passage or the ravages of time but the return of the past to our consciousness in such a way as to modify our awareness of the present. This reawakening of the past, lying dormant in our consciousness, is sparked off by some sense impression. Indeed sensation is an integral part of the process of recall, a process which is more passive than deliberate as far as Miró's characters are concerned, and which in a way belies the author's own recall of the past in this work, which of course takes the form of a deliberate and meticulous evocation. The role of the senses in transcending temporal barriers is shown to be crucial again and again. It is entirely as if Miró wishes to show that our senses do not recognize the conventions of time that govern our normal conscious lives. The 'sensación de presencia', the nowness of certain past experiences, affects several of the main characters at different times and in slightly different ways. At one point the adolescent Pablo is tempted by the orgy that the young rakes and servants have organized in don Amancio's house during his absence. Attracted yet repelled by the scene he is witnessing, he suddenly finds himself regressing in time to other sensual pleasures which he had experienced earlier as a schoolboy, and then he recalls the picture of St Godfrey which he had seen as a seven-year-old in the Bishop's rooms:

> Se vio y se sintió a sí mismo en instantes de sensualidad
> primorosa. (Mañana del último Viernes Santo. Palacio
> de Lóriz. Huerto florido en la madrugada de la Pasión
> del Señor. Rosales, azucenas, cipreses, naranjos, el árbol
> del Paraíso goteando la miel del relente. Hilos de agua
> entre carne de lirios. Y, dentro, salones antiguos que
> parecían guardados bajo un fanal de silencio; la estatua
> de doña Purita en un amanecer de tisús de retablo;
> mujeres que sólo al respirar besaban. Y por la noche, la
> procesión del Entierro; temblor de oro de luces; rosas
> deshojadas; la urna del Sepulcro como una escarcha de
> riquezas abriendo el aire primaveral, y él reclinado en
> suavidades: damascos, sedas, terciopelos; ambiente de

magnificencia, aromas de mujer y de jardines; tristeza
selecta de su felicidad; la luna mirándole, luna redonda,
blanca, como un pecho que le mantenía sus contenidos
deseos con delicia de acacias. Y viose más remoto, más
chiquito, delante de una estampa de la mesa de estudio
del prelado enfermo: la estampa de un niño cuya frente
de pureza eucarística, resiste el pico anheloso de un
avestruz, y ese niño, ya hombre, atormentado por
voraces tentaciones, murió virgen y puro.) La frente de
Pablo ardía desgarrada por pensamientos inmundos. (II,
p.344)

It is almost as if Pablo's past comes flooding back to him at that
crucial moment when he faces the decision of whether to join in the
base sensual pleasures which are beckoning, or whether to escape.
But it is clear that Miró is not presenting the experience as a stark
choice between sensual gratification and self-denial, despite St
Godfrey. Everything in the scene described is sensuous if not
sensual. The very attempt to ward off temptation is itself sensuous:
'Acogióse al recuerdo de lecturas y cuadros de apariciones de
ángeles que refrescan con sus alas las frentes elegidas; de vírgenes
coronadas de estrellas que mecen sobre sus rodillas, en el vuelo azul
de su manto, las almas rescatadas' (II, p.345). The experience of
coarse and sinful sexuality that lies before him brings back those
other experiences of a similar kind that had nevertheless been, not
distressing, but warm and reassuring. His turning to the 'claridades
y fragancias' of María Fulgencia instead of to the foul-smelling
debauchery ('vaho del refocilo') of the revellers is precisely a return
to his earlier experiences as recorded, stored, and re-played by the
senses.

As the instigator of memories of his childhood, the Bishop,
too, plays a key role in the life of the adolescent Pablo. When the
seventeen-year-old goes one day into the garden of the episcopal
palace impelled by a yearning to recover the lost innocence of his
childhood, he finds the Bishop, now a very sick man, who reminds
him of the time when he had first met him:

—¡No me tengas miedo! ¿Te acuerdas, Pablo? Así te
hablé la primera vez que, corriendo y jugando por todo
el Palacio, te asomaste a mi aposento. Te miraba jugar
desde mi ventana. Aquella tarde sentí que venías, y ni
me moví de mi sillón. Ahora también me estuve muy
quieto para que tampoco me tuvieses miedo.

La misma voz de entonces, pero más afligida. ¿No
era como la voz del Señor cuando reconviene al que se
aparta de su gracia? Todo niño se postró Pablo en la
tierra del tronco como antaño en la alfombra de la
biblioteca. (II, p.353)

It seems almost as if the Bishop has been waiting all these years for
such another afternoon. For his part Pablo, as he walks into the
garden, is transported by his sense impressions back to his
childhood: 'El niño de antes aleteó en Pablo y le pudo. Se dejaba
llevar de aquella interior criatura' (II, p.352). For Pablo the return
to the Bishop is a return to the innocence of childhood, an
innocence now disturbed by the cares of adolescence. In Pablo's
mind the Bishop is indelibly associated with the happiness and
enjoyment of his childhood hours in the episcopal palace. Returning
to the presence of the Bishop as a guilt-ridden adolescent, he at once
recovers his former gladness of spirit.

Paulina seems often aware of the hidden presence of the
Bishop, in contrast to Oleza, which, we are told, is aware only of his
absence, and she reminds her son of the Bishop's love for them:

—¡Cuántas veces, Pablo, te habrá bendecido sin que
tú te volvieses a su reja ni a su huerto, ese huerto tan
tuyo cuando eras chiquito!

Pablo hundió su sonrojo en la almohada.

Paulina recordó una lejana visita del prelado al
'Olivar'. Fue la tarde que don Alvaro le pidió por
esposa. El penitenciario, don Amancio y Monera
rodeaban a su padre, el abuelo Daniel, tan desvalido, tan

frágil, en el ancho sofá de la sala. Don Alvaro, en pie,
muy pálido, tenía en su mano un pomo de rosas, su
junco y su sombrero; el sol de los parrales le circulaba
por la frente. Apareció Su Ilustrísima, cuyos ojos
escudriñaban los corazones. A ella y su padre les sonrió,
dedicándoles las palabras del escudo del primer obispo
de Oleza: 'Llamad y se os abrirá'. (II, p.351)

For Paulina, too, the Bishop represents a possible way of coping
with the present through a return to the past. During the trauma
provoked by the affair of Pablo and María Fulgencia, Paulina,
unable to find solace before the Christ of the Holy Sepulchre or
before Our Father San Daniel, unable to turn to Father Bellod or to
Don Cruz, suddenly remembers the words of the Bishop uttered in
her own house of El Olivar some eighteen years earlier. And in
some mysterious way, of which even Paulina seems unaware, her
recollection brings her to the Bishop and puts her on the road to
happiness. The Bishop has had a relapse and Paulina cannot even
open her heart to him as Pablo had done a short time before. But
from his deathbed 'el llagado hablaba saliéndole un soplo de su
laringe podrida. Nadie le entendió. Cuando Paulina transpuso los
umbrales de Palacio, tampoco llevaba la salvación del hijo' (II,
p.362). But she is wrong; as soon as she arrives home she discovers
the miracle: Elvira has left and Don Alvaro decrees the return to her
childhood home for which she has yearned so much.[13]

   Towards the end of the novel the sense of the past, but also
perhaps of its irrecoverability, becomes even stronger. Pablo,
suddenly realizing that he is no longer a child, attributes this to a
new awareness of the past:

Eso sería no ser ya niño: depender del pasado sentir, de
su memoria, de sus acciones, de su conciencia, de los

---

[13]There is a possible echo here of the healing of the centurion's servant in
St Luke 7:6. Jesus performed the miracle at a distance, without the need to
go to the centurion's house.

instantes desaparecidos; proseguir el camino, rosigar el
pan de la víspera, acomodar la hora fina y tierna con la
hora cansada: sol, árboles, azul, aire del día nuevo, todo
ya con el regusto de nosotros según fuimos... (II, p.357)

The past is thus sensed by the mind with great vividness, yet is at
the same time ungraspable. Even future time is now perceived by
Pablo as an inevitable past: 'Hoy, a las doce y media, llevaría
veinticuatro horas sin besarla. ¡Mañana, dos días; y después, más
días y meses y meses!...' (II, p.359). Don Magín, too, sees everything as an irrecoverable past, even what has not yet passed. Citing
Jorge Manrique's *Coplas a la muerte de su padre*, the narrator,
seemingly speaking for don Magín, asks: '¿También lo no pasado lo
daremos por pasado?' (II, p.381). Time, Miró seems to imply, is an
illusory reality, a man-made convention which serves only to hide
the fact that we cannot experience it directly but only as past or as
future. Man has no real present; only memories and expectations.
Yet Miró does not stop at this ancient truism, although he appears
to subscribe to it. He goes further, and adds a much more modern
dimension to the concept of time: a psychological, subjective
perception of it.

The conventional view of time is that it is an absolute value
which exists independently of the observer. An alternative view, and
one which acquired currency, both scientific and artistic, in the
twentieth century, is that time is not an absolute but a convention
that allows society to share a common view of the order in which
things happen; beyond that convention individuals may experience
time differently, and in these subjective experiences chronological
time ceases to matter. Both social or conventional time and psychological or subjective time exist in this novel. Social time exists when
characters talk to each other about events that occurred in the past
and that serve to indicate elapsed time, for example when Don
Magín reminds Doña Corazón that it is exactly a year since Don
Vicente Grifol died. Social time is based on the clock and the
calendar and flows uninterruptedly in one direction only.
Psychological time is by contrast the experience not of society but of

a single individual, and each experience is unique and probably intransmissible. Psychological or subjective time can be completely different from clock time and need not be linear and unidirectional. It is this much less common notion of time that clearly interests Miró.

In many of the examples already discussed the past and present appear to merge in the consciousness of a character, and sometimes even the future is sensed as part of that same experience of time. Yesterday, today, tomorrow become one vast expanse. Time becomes a space that is inhabited all at once: '[...] esta tarde tan mía desde que era niña', says Paulina (II, p.205), implying that the present afternoon is still that same afternoon of old. For Paulina, of course, El Olivar becomes a mental refuge from her unhappy married life, and it is her emotional state that brings about her unusual perception of time.[14] The unhappiness which Paulina feels during the festivities of Holy Week described in *El obispo leproso*, at the moment when Máximo comes back into her life, makes her withdraw into her past to re-live a happiness which eludes her in the present. She cannot deny her present because she has a son whom she loves; but equally that perception of a youthful and romantic love, strongly rekindled by Máximo's reappearance in her life, the attractive thought of an alternative reality with him as her husband and as Pablo's father, blurs the distinction between the then and the now:

> Evidencia de una pena, de un amor, de una felicidad
> que se hubiera ya tenido en el instante que se produjo y
> en que nosotros no vivíamos. Sentirse en otro tiempo y
> ahora. La plenitud de lo actual mantenida de un lejano
> principio. Iluminada emoción de los días profundos de

---

[14]Marian Coope appears to believe that the opposite is the case, namely that it is the awareness of time that produces the state of mind (6, p.167). While I do not agree with this view, the important point, nevertheless, is that, whatever the explanation, a character's awareness of time as a complex or mysterious phenomenon is at its height during moments of emotional strain.

nuestra conciencia, los días que nos dejan, los mismos
días antepasados y conformados y que han de seguir
después de nuestra muerte. (II, p.229)

Paulina wills time to stand still, to stop but at a moment in her past,
and without sacrificing what she has in the present, i.e. Pablo. In a
quite unusual inversion of normal values, she desires not to retain
the past in the present, but the present in the past. The narrator's
mysterious comment in the final sentence of the passage just quoted
appears to suggest that these deep-felt emotions of ours become
timeless precisely because they are transferred from our subjective
consciousness to time itself, and time is one and imperishable. It is
not time that changes but only ourselves. The implication, although
Miró does not go so far as actually to say this, has to be that time is
present everywhere all of the time, and that it is not time that
governs change but change that creates the impression of the
passage of time: in an unchanging situation there is no flow of time,
merely an eternal moment.[15]

Miró's multifaceted exploration of the phenomenon of time is
further evinced by his treatment of the idea of elapsed time. Today
the science of psychology has amply documented that human
perception of time is not absolute and unchanging but can vary
according to an individual's situation and can thus be totally
independent of the clock. Not only does the human body have its
own biorhythms which do not coincide with time measured

---

[15]I agree with Marian Coope (6, p.176) when she says that time in Miró is
neither static nor fleeting but is simultaneously both; yet posing the
question in such traditional terms may not do justice to the complexity and
richness of Miró's treatment of the phenomenon. On another aspect of the
question my disagreement with Marian Coope is more fundamental. She
says that 'Miró describes change as a function of time' (6, p.135), whereas
I believe that, on the contrary, for Miró change is not a result of time but a
measure of it, i.e. that time is superficially perceived in terms of change;
but beyond that superficial perception there is a deeper perception of time
as an all-encompassing phenomenon that lies outside change and is
independent of it.

externally by the clock, but moreover a mental experience which may be subjectively conceived as lasting several hours can take place in a matter of minutes of objective, clock time. Dream states in particular, where the dreamer can have no awareness of clock time, can create huge discrepancies between subjective time and clock time; but even in a state of wakefulness research subjects deprived of access to clock time or other external indicators of objective time develop a sense of elapsed time which is substantially different from clock time. This altered, subjective, sense of elapsed time exists in the Oleza novels, and what is more it is planted by Miró even in the reader's mind. On several occasions we get the clear impression of a long passage of time when the clock has moved but little. As Marian Coope has pointed out, the acute stage of the Bishop's illness appears to last a very long time, but this is no more than an impression, created by Miró's description, for according to calendar time it lasts only a year. What Miró does is to break the natural chronology, to move the narrative back and forth imperceptibly, so that we never move forward without moving back; and, as we saw in chapter II, to use passages in the imperfect tense to create a sense of distance and of time flow:

> En todas las iglesias de la diócesis se rezaba por el llagado. El Señor le había elegido para salvar a Oleza. Y Oleza ya se cansaba de decirlo y oírlo. Oleza recordaba que el anterior prelado [...] no necesitó sufrir para obtener los bienes de su apostolado. Pues el otro pobre obispo de Alepo siquiera padecía por su perfección de santidad y no por redimir a nadie. ¿Ni redimir a estas horas de qué? Los hombres rubios pecadores, los extranjeros del ferrocarril, ya no estaban; y para los pecados del lugar no era menester una víctima propicia-toria.
>
> La víctima llevaba mucho tiempo escondida, sin audiencia, sin oficios ni galas; invisibles sus atributos, escasas las noticias de sus dolores [...].
>
> De los santos queda el culto, la liturgia, la estampa y

la crónica de su martirio. Del obispo leproso no se tenía
más que su ausencia, su ausencia sin moverse ya de lo
profundo de la ciudad, y el silencio y esquivez de su
casa entornada. Y al pasar por sus portales, las gentes
los miraban muy de prisa. (II, p.350)

As Marian Coope also explains, 'we are conditioned to think that
the Bishop's leprosy is of many years' duration, and this impression
is reinforced by the choice of images used to describe his palace' (6,
p.152). These images are contained in the mention of the new
spring grasses being allowed to invade the Bishop's abandoned
balcony, his furniture exuding 'un olor rancio de liturgia y de
eternidad' (II, p.245), and the old, discoloured sign outside his
office announcing the suspension of his audiences. The Bishop's
illness thus acquires a sense of timelessness, an apparent existence
outside the calendar of events. The effect of Miró's treatment of his
subject is to make the reader lose his sense of time, to see the
Bishop's illness not as an event in time but as a symbol above and
beyond the events that are occurring in Oleza. That Miró is deliberately manipulating reader reaction is further supported by his
deceptive association of suffering with redemption, the one occurring in time but the other for all time.

The altered perception of elapsed time affects not only the
reader but also the characters. It is a well-known phenomenon that
as human beings age time appears to pass much more quickly, and
additionally, that memory records less efficiently, so that recent
events may not be registered whereas distant, even childhood,
events can be recalled with great vividness. We have examples of
both of these phenomena in the Oleza novels. Doña Corazón, for
instance, from her vantage point of paralytic old age, says: '¡Ay,
todo pasa, todo pasa volando, don Magín!' (II, p.381). Don Magín,
though younger, agrees, and wonders if the future, too, will soon
have passed by as quickly as has the past. Don Vicente Grifol
remembers all kinds of minute details of distant events and people,
but can remember virtually nothing of what is going on in contemporary Oleza. He remembers Paulina's illness as a young girl, that

she had her hair cut on the Saturday before Palm Sunday and even what she wore to church the following day, but he cannot remember that she has got married only recently. Don Vicente is not unaware that time has moved on; it is simply that his mind can focus properly only on the events of the past, next to which the events of the present are a mere blur. Don Daniel, who is of a similar age to Don Vicente, is more aware of present events than is the doctor, but he sees them not as present or even as an immediate past but as a remote past. As the wedding party drives back to El Olivar after the ceremony Don Daniel turns to look at his daughter, 'y le pareció mucho tiempo casada' (I, p.185). And reviewing the events at El Olivar on the day of the betrothal immediately after the Bishop's departure from the scene, he feels those events to belong to a distant past: 'Todo lo acontecido lo veía muy lejos; todo había envejecido, en todos hallaba una sequedad de tránsito de mucho tiempo' (I, p.169). Mossén Orduña's problem on the other hand is that, absorbed as he is in his archaeological studies, he has little sense of time and cannot adjust quickly enough to the events that occur around him. Thus, when the news of the shooting of Don Magín penetrates his consciousness and he goes to Don Jeromillo's house to ask after the critically injured priest, a month or two have elapsed and the latter is well on the road to recovery.

The perception of time is virtually inseparable from the perception of sounds, fragrances, and even the objects surrounding the characters. Sounds have associations that take one back in time, indeed for Miró's characters it is not even the association but the sound by itself that seems to have this effect. When Don Daniel hears the church bells on the eve of St Peter's, the sound takes him back to his childhood, and Miró describes the phenomenon as if Don Daniel had physically regressed in time and was listening with the sensory faculties of the child: 'Y la esquila tocaba infantilmente' (I, p.29). For Don Magín, too, the church bell is a repository of time: 'Parece que le circule la sangre de las horas y de los toques de muchos siglos' (II, p.87). For Pablo the striking of the hours during the Good Friday service carries a much greater impact than the visual representation of the agony of Christ, or the preacher's sermon, or the sobs of contrite sinners, or the biblical account of the earthquake. It is the sounds of the bell that 'le precipitaron sus latidos en la dulce congoja de una verdad de belleza' (II, p.226). Fragrances are even more prominent, for the novel is suffused with olfactory sensations. Don Magín is of course the character with the greatest sensitivity to fragrances, and the sensuous scent of flowers becomes for him a substitute for other kinds of sense experiences which in his condition of priest he has chosen to forgo. Flowers smell of distant happiness: 'Casi siempre huelen las flores a un instante de felicidad que ya no nos pertenece', he says (I, p.208), and as he bids goodbye to Purita for the last time he thrusts a huge bunch of scented flowers into her lap in the realization that his happiness has truly gone forever. Paulina, too, senses in the fragrances of flowers and trees the scent of an ancient and promised happiness, a happiness of whose repossession she is uncertain but which she hopes will be transmitted to her son:

> Los jazmines, las rosas, los naranjos, los campos, el aire, la atmósfera de los tiempos de las viejas promesas, olor de felicidad no realizada, felicidad que Paulina sintió tan suya y que permanecía intacta en los jazmines, en el rosal, en los cipreses, en los frutales; la misma fragancia, la misma promesa que ahora recogía el hijo. (II, p.369)

Pablo for his part is too young to feel a sense of regret at unfulfilled expectations of happiness, though he too has had to suffer disappointments. As he returns at the end of the school year deeply upset at the absence of his mother from the prize-giving ceremony, the familiar smells of the town meet him as if he had been released from a long imprisonment in a remote place:

> Oleza, olorosa de ramajes para la procesión; vaho de pastelerías y de frutas de Corpus; aleteo de cobertores, aire de verano; goce de lo suyo, de lo suyo verdaderamente poseído, con perfume de los primeros jazmines,

> de canela y de ponciles. Todo el pueblo, todos los
> árboles, todas las gentes, parecía que perteneciesen a la
> heredad de Nuestro Padre; todo le acogía como si él
> volviese de profundas distancias. (II, p.278)

It is not just nature but inanimate objects too that have the power of
resurrecting the past in such a way as to affect us emotionally, to
mould our existence and to give us an identity and a sense of
belonging. By being taken away from El Olivar and enclosed in a
house full of alien objects and furniture Paulina is deprived of her
childhood security. Her unhappiness is associated with the objects of
her new environment, and the prospect of returning to El Olivar,
abandoning the objects of the Galindo household for those of her
childhood home, brings with it not just a memory of a distant past
but almost the conviction that a return to those familiar objects of
old will mean a return in time to a state of being that she lost when
she left:

> En El Olivar les esperaban los muebles suyos: las
> cómodas de olivo, los armarios de ciprés, los lechos de
> columnas de caoba, los candelabros de roca, los espejos
> románticos, las consolas, los relojes, los alabastros ... Y
> según iba recordando sus contornos, sus calidades, y
> pronunciándolo, adquirían configuraciones y semblante
> de vacilación. Todo aquello y los muros y envigados de
> los ámbitos de la casona y los árboles, la tierra y el aire
> y el silencio, todo pertenecía a su legítimo pasado, a su
> sangre, y, por tanto, a su hijo; todo estuvo aguardando la
> felicidad de la heredera desde antes que ella naciese. (II,
> p.363)

It is almost as if the furniture itself held the secret of time and therefore of happiness.

Occasionally an apparently trivial event is recalled in a
moment of stress and acquires a totally new significance. Such is
the case of Don Daniel and the *moscarda*. On the eve of St Peter

and St Paul, while visiting the cloisters of the cathedral after dining at his cousin's for what turns out to be the last time in his life, Don Daniel's contemplation of the building, its architecture, and its contents, is interrupted by the persistent buzzing of a *moscarda* or bluebottle, which he finds particularly unsettling and which he regards as an omen. Later that day during vespers and afterwards the memory of the fly haunts him. And it is while still thinking of the fly that he hears from Don Cruz the news of Don Alvaro's intention to ask for the hand of his daughter in marriage. A year later, completely deprived of the presence of his daughter, Don Daniel is dying. His eyes are fixed on a spot on a blank wall. Doña Corazón cannot at first understand why Don Daniel stares fixedly at the wall; but eventually Don Daniel points and Doña Corazón is able to make out his feeble efforts at speech: '¿Ves como no? ¡No es moscarda, no es! Es un clavo negro', she says (I, p.237). That nail that for the feverish don Daniel takes the form of the ominous fly also carries a further hidden association that of course escapes doña Corazón and Jimena:

> Y la Jimena añadió muy súbita:
> —Es la alcayata de aquel cuadro tan lindo que le regaló a Paulina el hermano de la condesa de Lóriz [...].
> Era un cuadro de una santa con el pecho desnudo. Se parecía a Paulina, y don Alvaro se lo llevó. (I, p.237)

Thus the fly that had bothered Don Daniel on that fateful day a year before when he first heard of Don Alvaro's intention, has now become the expression of Don Daniel's despairing sense of loss and abandonment. Behind that symbol lies the anguish of the dying man and his yearning for that earlier and happier time when he had his daughter (and the picture) by his side.

There is another incident which likewise acquires symbolic overtones, though this time of a more universal kind, and which similarly keeps recurring, not in Don Daniel's but in Paulina's mind. It is an incident which, like the Bishop's blessing of Paulina and Pablo commented on earlier, is not described independently at the time when it happened; it exists only as a recollection in the mind of a character. One Maundy Thursday, while Pablo was still very young and the family was visiting the churches in the traditional way, Don Alvaro had banged the boy's face against the feet of the statue of the dead Christ to make him kiss it, and in so doing had made his mouth bleed. The incident comes flooding back to Paulina many years later on another Maundy Thursday in front of the same dead Christ when she brings out the handkerchief — still showing the tell-tale bloodstains — with which she had cleaned her son's bleeding mouth. Later still, the episode is recalled when Don Alvaro, attempting to force a reluctant Pablo to kiss Elvira, pushes his face against his aunt's cheek. We can take it that the narrator, employing *style indirect libre*, is describing the scene through Paulina's mind, for it is she who reacts to the threat against her son that the memory of the earlier episode brings:

> Los ojos de don Alvaro daban el parpadeo de las ascuas.
> Y esos ojos le acechaban como la tarde del Jueves Santo,
> en que la boca del hijo sangró hendida por los pies
> morados del Señor. Paulina dio un grito de locura.
> ¡Sangre por el Señor, la ofrecía como martirio suyo;
> pero sangre de herida abierta por el hueso de aquella
> mujer la llagaría y marcaría siempre su vida! Y saltó
> desnuda del lecho, amparando al hijo. (II, p.281)

The episode is recalled for the third time when Paulina has wandered into the cathedral and in front of the chapel of the Holy Sepulchre trying to think to whom she could turn to help her son in his hour of need. The image of the dead Christ lies in front of her, cold, unwelcoming, and unconsoling, that same image 'en cuyos pies desollados y duros sangró la boca inocente de Pablo' (II, p.361). It is absolutely clear that in Paulina's subconscious the dead Christ is associated with Don Alvaro and others of the same religious ilk. This dead Christ offers no hope of salvation to Paulina. In a remarkable inversion of traditional Catholic symbolism, the dead Christ is made to stand for a religion based on fear, on punishment, and on a total absence of human warmth, feeling and under-standing. In this Miró is moving beyond the exploration of an individual consciousness and towards the denunciation of a whole inherited culture.

7. Theme and Ideology

Miró subtitled the first volume of the Oleza novels 'novela de capellanes y devotos' and in both it and its sequel the clergy plays a dominant role. Right from the opening pages Miró has chosen to emphasize the importance of religion and the influential position of the clergy in the life of Oleza. Oleza is described as first and foremost a clerical city: 'Oleza criaba capellanes como Altea merinos y Jijona turroneros', notes the narrator sardonically (I, p.76). The clergy and the religion which it purveys are not by and large — there are, of course, important exceptions — a force for the greater happiness and contentment of the inhabitants. Miró leaves no room for doubting that most of Oleza entertains a warped view of religion which in turn leads to a warped view of life. Miró's choice of Patron Saint is already significant, as Gerald Brown has shown (2, p.787): the Daniel of the Old Testament is an austere, self-righteous, even vindictive figure, obsessed by the thought that his people might succumb to the sensual pleasures of the Babylonians. But in case the reader fails to make the connection, Miró takes care to tell us what kind of saint the one represented by the statue of Oleza is. He is harsh and inflexible and his chief function is to punish those Olezans who indulge in carnal sins and to deter those others who might be tempted to succumb. His speciality is to uncover the sins of immoral maidens and unfaithful wives with his penetrating gaze. Needless to say, it is not the statue that Miró is characterizing but the popular conception of it. It is one more example of the way Miró speaks in this novel: by implication rather than by direct statement. He implies that in Oleza it is not God that counts but statues, San Daniel, Nuestra Señora del Molinar, the figure of Christ in the sepulchre. It is ironic — an intentional irony, no doubt — that when the word superstition is mentioned it is to deny its existence. 'Habló Don Cruz. Elogió el espectáculo de la fe

de un pueblo en su Patrono, sublime espectáculo de fervor en una
época de relajaciones, de falaces alarmas del "culto supersticioso de
las imágenes"' (I, p.109). The truth is very different, for superstition reigns supreme in Oleza. When a devout lady offers a tapestry
or mantle to the saint a rumour spreads that whoever touches the
cloth when the clock strikes three on the eve of the saint's feast will
obtain favours; at the appointed hour an unruly mob assaults the
church in a frenzied attempt to get at the miraculous cloth. A
recently married woman offers jewels to the statue of the Virgin so
that she will be blessed with children, but instead of offering her
best jewels she offers the cheap jewels given to her by her mother-
in-law; nine months later her mother-in-law gives birth. When the
Bishop's illness becomes public he is bombarded with all kinds of
infallible concoctions that are bound to bring about a cure, including
of course holy relics sent by religious foundations in the full expec-
tation that the miracle will occur. The distorted sense of religious
values is illustrated not only by these various anecdotes about super-
stitious belief and belief in absurd miracles, but also, and more
profoundly though more indirectly, by the general lack of positive
values in Oleza based on love for one's fellow humans. Of course
the Bishop, Purita, and Don Magín stand out as embodying the kind
of values, both religious and humanitarian, of which Miró silently
but evidently approves: a faith that is luminous, full of generosity
and of joy at natural things. But these characters, interesting in
themselves as they undoubtedly are, also serve a structural purpose:
they throw into greater relief, through an implied contrast, the
joyless and mean-spirited religion of clerical Oleza. For example,
Father Bellod and Don Magín, who represent opposing camps in
Oleza, are described, one as lacking a sense of smell and the other
as taking extreme delight in culinary and floral fragrances; or the
sounds of their footsteps as a 'pisar sonoro y limpio de bota
hebillada' (I, p.91) in Don Magín's case and as a 'chacoloteo de
almadreña' (I, p.204) in Father Bellod's case. The symbolic opposi-
tion between these two clergymen is brought to light by Miró's subtle
artistic contrivances but obeys a clear ideological motivation. The
novel is full of such implied contrasts. Miró scholars have pointed

out various examples: the contrasts between Don Alvaro and the Count, between, that is, the Carlist and the Liberal, the undemonstrative husband and the sensual husband, the stern, overbearing father and the tolerant, easy-going father; or the contrast between the man Paulina marries and her adolescent love, the romantic Máximo. But there is, in the case of Alvaro, another more subtle and revealing contrast: that between him and the Bishop. The associations between the two men, though barely hinted at, are too numerous to be a coincidence. Here are just some of them: they arrive in Oleza at the same time and immediately take a dislike to each other; they are both attracted to Paulina and in a strange way they are rivals, a rivalry intimated as early as the scene in which the Bishop interrupts the engagement ceremony: Don Alvaro has gone to El Olivar to ask for Paulina's hand in marriage, but it is the Bishop who 'escogió las manos de la doncella' (I, p.166) an apparently harmless phrase that in the context in which it occurs is pregnant with implication, for it marks the start of the triangular relationship Bishop-Paulina-Don Alvaro. And very much later it is the Bishop's intervention that will save El Olivar for Paulina when Don Alvaro wants to give it away. Don Alvaro, the husband who should openly express his love for Paulina, cannot do so because of his emotional frigidity, whereas the Bishop, who cannot do so because of his position, nevertheless finds it possible to convey to her his secret blessing, which Paulina gratefully receives and treasures for the rest of her life. Both men think frequently of Paulina, but how differently! Alvaro can only think of her as a temptation to sexual indulgence and is obsessed by the terrifying though entirely hypothetical thought of what his wife might be like in another man's arms; the Bishop, on the other hand, is able to think of Paulina during 'tantos años sin sonrojarse de ninguno de sus pensamientos' (II, p.354). That Paulina should represent sin for the husband yet pure love for another man is an extraordinary paradox, and one that Miró uses to suggest that sin is not so much an act as an attitude of mind. Don Alvaro's mentality is dominated by the concept of sin to such a degree that he cannot give his wife the natural affection of a spouse; but the Bishop can love Paulina virtuously because his mind is pure. The contrast goes even further. The Bishop is Pablo's father too, a surrogate father to whom Pablo flees from his real father and who plays with and entertains the child as Don Alvaro never does. And indeed it is to the Bishop that the adolescent Pablo turns for consolation in a moment of crisis. Don Alvaro's physical enemy is Cara-rajada, but beyond him Don Alvaro sees the Bishop, who is Cara-rajada's protector: 'le complacía juntarlos en su pensamiento' (I, p.223). Don Alvaro fears Cara-rajada not because he poses a physical threat but because he knows of Don Alvaro's act of moral cowardice, a shameful weakness in a man who prides himself on his moral integrity. And Don Alvaro sees the Bishop as an enemy for precisely the same reason: the Bishop has seen through the hollowness of his moral uprightness. In all this Miró is certainly subtle, but the artistic subtlety serves an ideological purpose.

The use of contrastive parallelism is one of Miró's most favoured techniques in this novel, and some of the many examples are not immediately obvious. The Bishop's concern for the welfare of his pigeons, of which we learn in passing during a scene in which Father Bellod is vexed at suffering an interruption by the Bishop's columbine preoccupation, functions as a contrast to Bellod's own appallingly sadistic treatment of the rook. Whereas the Bishop is shown to have a love for animals and of nature, Bellod, who in matters of religious and social ideology does not share the Bishop's progressive outlook, is characterized as entertaining an attitude of contempt and animosity towards the natural world. Many of the contrastive parallels in the novel have to do with character, as does so much else in this novel so rich in characterization. But their real function is not the surface one of character portrayal. For example, the various structural parallels between the Galindo family and the Lóriz family point to the latter having been conceived precisely as a contrast to the former: simultaneous marriages; simultaneous pregnancies (one hidden from the public, the other publicly proclaimed); the two families residing on opposite sides of the same street, in houses that are reinhabited at the same time, one with shutters permanently closed, the other with shutters permanently open, etc. What Miró is doing through the use of those contrastive parallels is illustrating how two similar situations — in this case marriage and family life — can have totally different outcomes according to the religious philosophy that informs those families. Thus, family life for the Galindos turns out to be claustrophobic, strained, and deeply unhappy, whereas for the Lórizs it is open, relaxed, and fulfilled. Miró does not tell us in so many words why things turn out this way; but the way in which he presents the situations invites these inferences to be made.

Another telling contrast, even though a more obvious one, is that between Elvira and Purita. One represents rampant sexuality, the other unsullied decency. But which is which? It emerges that Miró's view of these two women is precisely the reverse of Oleza's view of them. It is Elvira, the puritan, who comes to personify sexual depravity, while Purita, the most desirable woman in Oleza and the constant butt of malicious gossip and insinuations, considered 'demasiado libre' to make a good wife, turns out to be chaste. Whereas Elvira's unnatural purity provokes nausea ('bascas de pureza', writes Miró ironically), Purita's natural sexuality provokes admiration and joy, at least in those not tainted with the lugubrious religious philosophy of clerical Oleza. Elvira sees herself and is seen by others as sacrificing herself for the sake of her brother's family; but we are left in no doubt by Miró that the truly generous and self-sacrificing nature belongs to Purita, and, when, resigned to the spinsterhood to which puritanical Oleza has condemned her, she leaves for Valencia to look after her nephews, Miró puts words in her mouth which are full of significance: 'Ya no me quedo para vestir imágenes: voy a vestir, y lavar, y besar sobrinos que dan gloria' (II, p.384). The implication is that a society as levitical and narrow-minded as that of Oleza, a society in which religious statues count for more than people, has no use for those positive human qualities based on joy, warmth, and affection. Purita's departure is not just Don Magín's loss but Oleza's. Oleza is left to her cult of wooden idols as her most vibrant and wholesome daughter leaves for good. It is interesting that Purita's departure follows closely on the heels of Elvira's: at the moment when Elvira's disgrace prevents her from looking after her nephew as she had pretended to be doing all along, Purita goes off to look after hers for real. It seems entirely likely that Purita's much-expanded role in *El obispo leproso* arose from Miró's desire to provide an ideological contrast to Elvira. Elvira constantly decries sexual sin, but she is herself motivated by a warped sexuality. Purita is totally natural in the expression of her female personality and physique, is not obsessed with sin, and despite the malevolent insinuations of those who are envious of her beauty, remains chaste. Elvira is cheerless and incapable of enjoying life or of irradiating joy. Purita is full of joie de vivre and has the knack of imparting her sense of joy to others. It is not to be doubted that Miró has fully intended to embody two contrasting attitudes to life in these two characters; nor is it in the slightest bit necessary to spell out which one we are invited to extol and which one to condemn. Miró's art makes his message abundantly clear.

Beyond the individual personalities of the characters there is Oleza society itself. There are, as we have seen, several aspects of this society and of its religion that Miró satirizes, but the picture is at its bleakest in everything that brings religion and sex together, that is, in everything that concerns the idea of purity. Purity for many Olezans is in fact puritanism of the most inhuman kind. In the name of purity a young mother is virtually locked away and separated from her father, her son, and her relatives; in the name of purity a dying man is deprived of the comfort of his only daughter; in the name of purity a mother is stopped from kissing her son by a priest; in the name of purity people who do not conform to enforced clerical standards of austerity and asceticism are subjected to a vitriolic and merciless character-assassination; and so on and so forth. Miró harps so constantly on this same notion that the list of examples is endless. 'Puro', according to Don Cruz, is Alvaro, but his purity does not prevent him either from being tyrannical or from wanting to enjoy, but being incapable of enjoying, the sexual attractions of his wife. In Don Alvaro Miró has given us an embodiment of the confused and harmful religious ideal that identifies purity with sexual repression. The way in which Don Alvaro has learnt to repress his feelings produces not Christian love or virtue, but a sterile excitation that only leads to others' unhappiness as well as his own. The same distorted ideal of purity is held by Elvira and by other women of Oleza. They too are under the delusion that their purity is a guarantee of true religious affiliation and a sign of virtue. They are scandalized because the Countess dares to go out in the street parading her pregnancy. For them this is an act of indecency because her pregnancy reminds them of the sexual act that preceded it, and this act is deemed to be repugnant: as the narrator puts it, reflecting what is going on in the mind of Elvira, 'un hijo, de lo primero que sirve, es de malicia para llevar la cuenta de pasadas satisfacciones en que fue engendrado' (I, p.264). Their abhorrence of everything sexual even extends to the natural world: 'este olor de acacias, de naranjos [...] es un olor de perdición' (I, p.264). Their virtuous spirits in fact move in a murky zone where lurk unsatisfied and unrecognized desires. When Purita, from the innocence of her seventeen years, remarks that she would like to get married, the virtuous women experience 'un frío de horror voluptuoso' (I, p.265). What Miró appears to be hinting at with this striking phrase is that their repugnance is itself sinful because they derive an inverted pleasure from it.

The Jesuits, too, come in for a subtle form of criticism on those same grounds. The hatred of Miró's Jesuits for all things sensual is at its peak in everything connected with sex. When attending religious acts, school ceremonies and school plays, parents and relatives have to observe strict sexual separation under the vigilance of a Brother Inspector. And woe betide those who indulge in the slightest infringement of these laws of conduct which do not permit even an admiring look or a friendly smile between persons of the opposite sex! Don Roger and Señor Hugo have their contracts rescinded because they made Doña Purita laugh with delight during the school reception on the festivity of Corpus Christi, an infringement that did not escape the ever watchful eye of Father Prefect, spying 'desde la sombra del séptimo pilar del claustro' (II, p.275). Invited by the Lórizs to come to the palace accompanied by the older pupils to watch the Good Friday processions, the Reverend Fathers take exception to the atmosphere of jollity among the young women of the house. Pablo, who partakes of that joviality, is punished for his misconduct, only to be quickly forgiven by Father Prefect with evident satisfaction when he falsely accuses the women. By turning on the women Pablo is recognizing the adversary, and the adversary is for the Jesuits sensuality and those who indulge in it, but a sensuality so defined that it embraces any manifestation of warmth and endearment. The Society of Jesus sees sensuality at every turn. Oleza is, in the eyes of Father Spiritual, a pit of sensuality: 'Es la hora de decir al Maestro: ¡Baje fuego y consuma Samaria! Oleza es Samaria' (II, p.272). The excessive austerity of the Jesuits in everything that concerns the natural expression of affection, their consequent coldness and lack of understanding towards those persons who express their feelings openly, is an aspect that does not escape Miró's implied criticism. '¡No podían vivir sin quererse, sin besarse, sin tocarse! ¡Oh, qué engaños y peligros tenían los alumnos en sus familias; y singularmente en la madre, en la madre y en las hermanas!' (II, p.227), thinks Brother Janitor when the families of boarders come to visit the pupils. And when Paulina comes on Good Friday, after her son's punishment, to console him with a kiss, the Brother separates them saying: '¡En esta tarde Nuestra Señora no pudo besar a su Hijo sino después de muerto!' (II, p.228).

That Oleza is rather more than a faithful reconstruction of provincial Orihuela in the 1890s, that it functions as a symbol of traditional Catholic Spain, is suggested not only by its close association — insisted upon by Miró — with Carlists and Jesuits, but also and above all by the inclusion of certain references which hark back to an earlier age and which have the effect of associating clerical Oleza with sixteenth-century Spain. The beginnings of Oleza, we are told in *Nuestro Padre San Daniel*, are firmly rooted in the Spain of Philip II, who happens to be the monarch responsible for appointing the first bishop of Orihuela. We are also informed that the statue of the Prophet Daniel, which clearly symbolizes the puritanical and austere outlook of the Olezans, was sculpted between 1580 and 1600 and that the first miracles date also from that time, a time of great religious intensity under that intensely

religious monarch Philip II. Another association with the sixteenth
century occurs when the Carlist envoy makes his appearance, for
Don Alvaro is presumed by some to be the illegitimate son of the
Carlist Pretender, an explicit parallel being established with King
Charles I of Spain and his illegitimate son Don John of Austria,
Philip II's half-brother. In this way Don Alvaro is associated with
the king notorious in history for his religious intransigence and
persecution of those who deviated from the strictest orthodoxy.
Father Bellod, a member of Don Cruz's and Don Alvaro's coterie
and a kindred spirit, is implicitly associated with the institution
which did so much to promote religious intolerance under Philip II:
the Inquisition. At precisely that instant when Doña Corazón is
entertaining thoughts on the Trinity that border on the heterodox,
though no less innocuous for that, Father Bellod puts in an appearance with his penetrating gaze, his harsh words, and his accusatory
'índice sacerdotal', Miró's ingenious play on *índice* associating the
accusation of today with the prohibition of yesteryear. Don Magín,
on the other hand, not only makes light of the whole thing but
moreover expounds upon the historical phenomenon of heresy as if
it were the most natural thing in the world. All this has the effect of
evoking a historically identifiable Spain with strong religious
affiliations and of associating contemporary Oleza with that Spain.
The Oleza of Father Bellod and Don Alvaro is, like the Spain of
Philip II, one in which religious fanaticism, intolerance of dissenting views, and obsession with social and moral conformity produce
an atmosphere of spiritual claustrophobia, suspicion, and denigration.

   Nor was Miró alone in establishing this connection between
contemporary and sixteenth-century Spain. The need for a spiritual
regeneration of Spain was a recurrent theme of the early twentieth-
century writers known collectively as the Generation of 1898. This
spiritual regeneration necessitated the rejection of a religious
mentality which the *noventaiochistas* traced back to Habsburg
Spain. These writers — among them most insistently Miguel de
Unamuno — saw in the Spain of the sixteenth century the
beginnings of a Catholicism that was unthinking, monolithic, and

repressive, the beginnings, that is, of the spiritual impoverishment of the nation that still affected Spain at the beginning of the twentieth century.[16] But from among the wreck of Spanish sixteenth-century spirituality some figures were deemed worthy of rescue, none more so than the poet and theologian Fray Luis de León. In Fray Luis, Unamuno saw the embodiment of a Platonic humanism that, had it not been extirpated by the Inquisition, would have brought forth a spirituality very different from that which actually took root in Spain. Unamuno highlights Fray Luis's deep feeling for the natural world, for nature is seen as the reflection of an ideal world of peace and harmony.[17] It is precisely this aspect of Fray Luis that also struck a fellow-member of the 1898 Generation, Azorín, who wrote: 'El escritor será tanto más artista cuanto mejor sepa interpretar la *emoción del paisaje* [...]. Es una emoción completamente, casi completamente moderna. En Francia sólo data de Rousseau y Bernardino de Saint Pierre [...]. En España, fuera de algún poeta primitivo yo creo que sólo la ha sentido Fray Luis de León en sus Nombres de Cristo.'[18] Here we have an interesting point of contact with Miró, who, like Unamuno and Azorín, evinced a particular predilection for the writings of this sixteenth-century figure.[19] It transpires that Miró's Don Magín has a significant amount in common with the Fray Luis admired by the *noventaiochistas*, a lover of nature and a victim of the 'sociedad de lobos' (in Unamuno's phrase) in which it was his fate to live. Fray Luis was an Augustinian, while Don Magín has a picture of St

---

[16]Unamuno writes in one place: 'Estamos aún expiando aquel crimen de haber querido ahogar el renacimiento del espíritu cristiano en Europa' (*Obras completas*, IX (Madrid: Escelicer, 1971), p.116). And in another place: 'Aún hay hoy menos libertad íntima que en la época de nuestro *fanatismo* proverbial' (I, (1966), p.866).

[17]See in particular *En torno al casticismo*, part IV, chapter 3.

[18]Azorín, *La voluntad*, ed. E. Inman Fox, Clásicos Castalia, 4 (Madrid: Castalia, 1968), pp.291–92.

[19]Miró's fondness for Fray Luis de León is attested by Ian Macdonald (*14*, pp. 93–94 and 138–39). It should be added that the *noventaiochistas*' view of Fray Luis was coloured by the fact that he had suffered at the hands of the religious establishment.

Augustine in his room. Like Fray Luis, Don Magín is described as a Renaissance figure; he is a classicist in his historico-literary preferences, devoted to the study of antiquity and the biblical world, and an expert on ecclesiastical history; his Catholicism is a shade heterodox, since he devotes himself to 'indagaciones desconsoladoras', as the Bishop labels them (I, p.198); he longs to visit the Biblical lands, which he knows only through his studies; he suffers persecution, if not as did Fray Luis at the hands of the Inquisition, which no longer exists, at any rate at the hands of an inquisitorial Carlist and Jesuitical Oleza which makes odious and false accusations against him and which, perhaps symbolically, almost deprives him of his life in an inflamed exhibition of bellicose self-assertion; and he is, above all, a profound lover of the natural world, the landscape, the fruits and flowers, the sun and the night sky, and the fragrances of the harvest carried on the wind. The parallelism is strongly suggestive, and it is entirely plausible that Miró was thinking of Fray Luis de León when he conceived the figure of this congenial priest who under the guise of a Renaissance humanist embodies the *noventaiochista* ideal of a humanized and universal *homo religiosus*.

Miró's critique of the religion of Oleza does not rest solely on its association with the dehumanized orthodoxy of Philip II's Spain. There are further aspects of his implicit criticism of Spanish Catholicism which, although oblique, are disturbing and profound. The image of Christ that is most frequently invoked in the novel is that of the Holy Sepulchre, of the entombed Christ. The Christ is a dead Christ, a Christ who turns to look only at Paulina (I, p.271 and II, p.231), who is herself the victim of an opressive religion and of a husband who, held up as a 'caballero cristiano' (I, p.134), locks her up, entombs her, in the name of chastity. At this point Miró's religious critique, with its ironic inversion of values, reaches unsuspected levels of subtlety, and there is a complex web of implicit associations not easy to unravel, but which suggests a conscious strategy of undermining what he considers to be objectionable aspects of Spanish Catholicism and its influence. Both ideologically and socially, Don Alvaro belongs to Father Bellod's circle. Father Bellod entertains ideas on matrimony of such austerity that they border on the hostile; he represents a particular vision of marriage which has enjoyed a strong tradition within the Church: marriage as an institution to be tolerated in so far as it fulfils the need to propagate the human species, but which attains a much greater degree of acceptability and perfection when it exists in a state of complete sexual abstinence. Father Bellod's hostility towards marriage, because it renders licit what for him should always be illicit — sexual relations or, as he puts it, 'las indignidades del matrimonio' (I, p.75) — and his constant exaltation of virginity, are very clearly depicted throughout the novel, but in addition we are given a list of women saints who chose martyrdom rather than lose their virginity and of Christian marriages which either were not consummated or else soon evolved into purely spiritual unions, with the complete renunciation of conjugal rights. If we bear in mind that Don Alvaro fully shares the ideas of Father Bellod and that moreover it is the latter who officiates at his friend's wedding, one cannot escape the conclusion that Miró is offering us the marriage of Don Alvaro and Paulina as a modern and vivid example of that kind of Christian marriage so dear to the religious tradition represented by Father Bellod. This marriage, Don Cruz tells Father Bellod, in an attempt to overcome the austere priest's aversion, 'era también el origen de una sangre nueva en la perfección del ideal cristiano' (I, p.186). It later transpires, however, that this exemplary Christian marriage is a failure and a source of misery for the spouses; and it is a failure because it is subjected to norms of conduct which, though outwardly Christian, are in fact brutally oppressive. The allusions to the sexual frustrations of Don Alvaro and the amorous fantasies of Paulina allow us to infer that after the birth of their son there has been no sexual relation between husband and wife, but instead of reinforcing the spiritual bond between the spouses as Father Bellod's tradition of the Christian marriage would have it, all that this achieves is to submerge them in an inhospitable atmosphere of harshness, moodiness, and tension. The religious ideals to which Don Alvaro wishes to subject his marriage end by almost destroying it, by which Miró gives us to understand that the ideal of a virginal marriage is a clerical distortion and an unhealthy and unnatural one, an idea further supported by the failure of the other virginal marriage in this novel, that between Don Amancio and María Fulgencia. Miró's religious critique becomes even sharper if we bear in mind the subtle irony with which the novelist associates Don Alvaro's marriage with the failure of a gloomy and stifling religion. It is here that the full significance of the dead Christ, the entombed Christ of the Holy Sepulchre, who so often makes an appearance, can be appreciated. Paulina goes to her wedding dressed not in white, as both she and we expected, but in black, as if she were attending a funeral. And in the final scene of *Nuestro Padre San Daniel*, in which she visits the Church of Nuestro Padre, and in which among the images described are those of the interred Christ and of *el ahogao* stripping himself of his sanctity 'como un hombre cansado, muy triste, se va quitando su sonrisa y su vestidura en su dormitorio' (I, p.272), we observe Paulina experiencing 'la angustia del enterrado vivo' (I, p.272), a sensation and a language which drive home the ideological function of the complex relationship of images, references and incidents. Don Alvaro is associated with death, and in particular with the dead Christ (the Holy Week procession in which he is an active participant is precisely that of the Santo Entierro). For Paulina, her wedding turns out, retrospectively, to have been a funeral, and her marriage an entombment, due of course to the regime to which her husband and sister-in-law subject her, they being in turn unwitting victims of their blind adhesion to an implacable and baneful Christianity which ruins their lives. But in addition to making Don Alvaro share the religious ideas of Don Cruz and Father Bellod, Miró raises the story of Paulina's family from the anecdotal to the symbolical and forces us to an inescapable conclusion. The religion that these characters adhere to (and we must not forget that it is the religion of Oleza as a whole) is a dead religion, that is, a religion which is anti-vital, destructive of the love for one's fellow-humans and for life itself, resistant to social emancipation and progress, and fastened onto a sombre and melancholy way of life. Miró's condem nation of the religious values of traditional Catholic Spain is undeclared yet profound.

One qualification, however, needs to be made. Miró's criticism is directed not against religion itself but against a particular conception of it: religion as a prohibitive, suppressive, coercive, and comminatory instrument. For if on the one hand we have Don Alvaro, Don Cruz and Father Bellod trying to put shackles on every inhabitant to make them conform to their own narrow views, we have on the other Don Magín and the Bishop, who evidently embody an authorial vision of religion as something positive and commendable. The Bishop disdains the religious formulae and external trappings so dear to clerical Oleza, but on the other hand takes a personal interest in the welfare of the most humble of his diocesans, as is made clear through numerous examples. Don Magín has no time for 'la virtud andrajosa y sudada como la del Padre Bellod' (I, p.94) and pays no heed to the hypocritical gossip of the small-minded clerical lobby of Oleza; for him, religion has no quarrel with nature, and the enjoyment of the latter is both legitimate and beneficial. Just like the Bishop, Don Magín looks after the less fortunate. The friendship which unites these two characters, one based on mutual respect and not on group identity, their scholarly interest in matters of ancient history, their unconcern for matters of mere etiquette, their tolerance and their adherence to more purely human values, their independence of mind and of conduct, contrast strongly with the behaviour and attitude of the other Oleza, thereby giving us some idea of the kind of religious ideology advocated by Miró, a religion that is ethical and not dogmatic, life-enhancing rather than enslaving, free from superstition and overflowing with joy at the things of nature.

That Miró is castigating the society of provincial Spain in the closing decades of the last century is incontestable. But too exclusive an emphasis on the geographical and temporal setting of the work and the allusions to the Orihuela of Miró's youth runs the risk of overlooking the concepts that underlie the portrayal of a society at a specific historical moment. Miró's theme is not just provincial Spain in 1900 but religious fanaticism and the havoc it can wreak, a timeless phenomenon that belongs both in the past and in the present and affects very different societies. Miró of course presents the problem in its Spanish dimension. Thus what the Oleza novels amount to, from an ideological perspective, is a denunciation and repudiation of that brand of Catholicism which had flourished in Spain since the time of Ferdinand and Isabella: a Catholicism which demanded unthinking allegiance to rigidly defined norms, which bred intolerance of dissenting views, which condemned the enlightened humanism of Erasmus and his many Spanish followers, and whose obsession with sins of the flesh fostered a society characterized by sexual repression and its negative effects. Quietly but implacably Miró denounces the spiritual philosophy of those who would create a vengeful, austere and sombre God, a God based on their own pettiness, gloomy view of life, and contorted sense of virtue. Theirs is the God of a fanatical people lacking in charity and understanding, a real enough God for Miró and one to be feared: '¡Más puro y rígido el Dios de don Alvaro que el mismo don Alvaro! ¡Ay, don Magín, y qué Dios tan terrible! ¡Dios nos libre de ése!' (II, p.184), says the wise old maidservant Jimena. But through the quasi-pantheistic Don Magín, Miró offers us a glimpse of a different God, a God who escapes the clutches of those narrow minds of clerical and Carlist Oleza: 'Por mucho que los hombres se afanen, y entre todos Don Alvaro, en invocar a un Dios que se les parezca, Dios es siempre mejor que ellos, por fortuna para los bienaventurados' (II, p.183). The invitation is to reject the apocalyptic God of punishment and death and follow instead the God of love and life.

Bibliographical Note

1. Alfred W. Becker, *El hombre y su circunstancia en las obras de Gabriel Miró* (Madrid: Revista de Occidente, 1958). A general study on the theme of Miró's characters and their problems; still useful though limited.

2. Gerald G. Brown, 'The Biblical Allusions in Gabriel Miró's Oleza Novels', *Modern Language Review*, 70 (1975), 786–94. An important essay on Miró's use of biblical parallels and allusions, at times speculative but always suggestive.

3. Rodolfo Cardona, 'Tradición e innovación en *Nuestro Padre San Daniel*', in *Harvard University Conference in Honor of Gabriel Miró*, ed. Francisco Márquez Villanueva (Cambridge, MA.: Harvard University, 1982), pp.47–61. A rather diffuse essay which argues that Miró's subject is traditional but his treatment of it very up-to-date in its techniques.

4. Marian G.R. Coope, 'Gabriel Miró's Image of the Garden as *Hortus Conclusus* and *Paraíso Terrenal*' *Modern Language Review*, 68 (1973), 94–104. A good essay which rightly emphasizes the role and importance of garden settings in the Oleza novels.

5. ——, 'The Critics' View of *Nuestro Padre San Daniel* and *El obispo leproso* by Gabriel Miró', in *University of British Columbia Hispanic Studies*, ed. H. V. Livermore (London: Tamesis, 1974), pp.51–60. An informative article on the critical reception of the Oleza novels with corrective comments on the critics' misjudgements.

6. ——, *Reality and Time in the Oleza Novels of Gabriel Miró* (London: Tamesis, 1984). A detailed and essential study of Miró's sources of inspiration.

7. ——, 'La insignificancia de don Vicente Grifol y la teoría novelística de Gabriel Miró', *Revista Canadiense de Estudios Hispánicos*, 12 (1987–88), 17–31. Argues that Miró expresses his literary ideas through this particular personage.

8. Ricardo Gullón, 'Oleza y sus gentes', in *Critical Essays on Gabriel Miró*, ed. R. López Landeira (Ann Arbor: Society of Spanish and Spanish-American Studies, 1979), pp.138–44. Also, with minor differences, in *La invención del 98 y otros ensayos* (Madrid: Gredos, 1969), pp.113–25. A rather diffuse essay (the original version dating back to 1952), but with valuable insights.

9. ——, 'La novela lírica', in *Homenaje a Gabriel Miró: estudios de crítica literaria*, ed. J. L. Román del Cerro (Alicante: Publicaciones de la Caja de Ahorros Provincial, 1979), pp.15–34. Reprinted in *La novela lírica*, I: *Azorín y Miró. El escritor y la crítica*, ed. Darío Villanueva (Madrid: Taurus, 1983), pp.243–58. A brilliantly suggestive (and debatable) attempt to classify *El obispo leproso* as a lyrical novel by analysing Miró's original treatment of his characters' perception and expression of emotions.

10. Roberta Johnson, 'Miró's *El obispo leproso*: Echoes of Pauline Theology in Alicante', *Hispania*, 59 (1976), 239–46. A somewhat forced reading of *El obispo leproso* as an allegory of St Paul's moral teaching, but with many perceptive points in passing.

11. Edmund L. King, 'Gabriel Miró y "el mundo según es"', *Papeles de Son Armadans*, 62 (1961), 121–42. Reprinted in *La novela lírica*, I (see 9), pp.205–16. A pioneering essay on Miró's art which argues that this phrase of Miró's reveals his aesthetic and moral attitude.

12. ——, Introduction to his edition of Gabriel Miró, *Sigüenza y el Mirador Azul y Prosas de El Ibero* (Madrid: Ediciones de la Torre, 1982). Miró's reply to Ortega's criticism (see 25): important for the insight it provides into Miró's aesthetics.

13. P.A. López Capestany, '*Nuestro Padre San Daniel*, novela psicológica', *Cuadernos Hispanoamericanos*, 275 (July, 1973), 349–59. Argues that *Nuestro Padre San Daniel* is above all a psychological novel: what predominates is the characters' internal tensions.

14. Ian Macdonald, *Gabriel Miró: His Private Library and his Literary Background* (London: Tamesis, 1975). An important study, essential for a proper understanding of Miró's literary formation.

15. ——, 'Gabriel Miró: el novelista creador de sí mismo', *Insula*, 392–93 (July–Aug. 1979), 8. On Miró's idea of happiness as embodying a conscious choice of path in life.

16. ——, '"Caminos y lugares": Gabriel Miró's *El obispo leproso*', *Modern Language Review*, 77 (1982), 606–17. A perceptive essay which explores the theme of the journey as a spatial metaphor of the characters' development.

17. ---, 'Why is Miró's Bishop a Leper?', *Anales de la Literatura Española Contemporánea*, 7 (1982), 59–77. Throws a good deal of light on a very basic question.

18. Francisco Márquez Villanueva, 'La esfinge mironiana', in *Harvard University Conference* (see 3), pp.11–34. A good general essay on the aesthetic position of Miró.

19. Yvette Miller, *La novelística de Gabriel Miró* (Madrid: Códice, 1975). A competent and useful study of technical aspects of the Oleza novels, with special emphasis on Miró's 'elliptical technique'.

20. ——, 'Illusion of Reality and Narrative Technique in Gabriel Miró's Oleza-Orihuela Novels', in *Critical Essays* (see *8*), pp.57–65. In Spanish in *La novela lírica*, I (see *9*), pp.266–75. Summarizes the main findings of *19*.

21. Enrique Moreno Báez, 'El impresionismo de *Nuestro Padre San Daniel*', in *Studia philologica: homenaje a Dámaso Alonso*, II (Madrid: Gredos, 1961), pp.493–508. Reprinted in *La novela lírica*, I (see *9*), pp.276–91. Identifies many important characteristics of Miró's prose style and presentation but seriously underestimates capacity for character portrayal.

22. Paciencia Ontañón de Lope, 'Gabriel Miró, espíritu del 98', in *Studia hispánica in honorem R. Lapesa*, III (Madrid: Gredos, 1975), pp.375–86. Rightly insists on Miró's censure of provincial life and religion and sees a parallel with the social criticism of the Generation of 1898.

23. ——, 'Realidad y patología de un personaje mironiano', in *Critical Essays* (see *8*), pp.145–50. A semi-Freudian analysis of Elvira Galindo.

24. ——, *Estudios sobre Gabriel Miró* (México: UNAM, 1979). A varied collection of useful essays which includes the two preceding entries.

25. José Ortega y Gasset, '*El obispo leproso*, novela, por Gabriel Miró', *Obras completas*, III, 4th ed. (Madrid: Revista de Occidente, 1957), pp.544–50. An influential, but negative and uncomprehending, early book review (written 1927). For Miró's reply, see *12*.

26. Susan O'Sullivan, 'Watches, Lemons and Spectacles: Recurrent Images in the Works of Gabriel Miró', *Bulletin of Hispanic Studies*, 44 (1967), 107–21. A good follow-up article to L. J. Woodward (*32*) throwing further light on Miró's imagery.

27. Rosa Perelmuter Pérez, 'Hermetismo y expansión en dos novelas de Gabriel Miró', *Hispanófila*, 68 (Jan. 1980), 47–56. A useful study showing how Miró's characters can be divided into those who love open spaces and those who prefer enclosed spaces.

28. Vicente Ramos, *Gabriel Miró* (Alicante: Instituto de Estudios Alicantinos, 1979). The standard biography.

29. Manuel Ruiz-Funes, Introduction to his edition of *Nuestro Padre San Daniel* (Madrid: Ediciones Cátedra, 1988). An excellent annotated edition with glossary and a usefully informative introduction. See also *36*.

30. Carlos Ruiz Silva, Introduction to his edition of *Nuestro Padre San Daniel* (Madrid: Ediciones de la Torre, 1981). A good annotated edition (used throughout this Guide) with a glossary and an excellent introduction.

31. ——, Introduction to his edition of *El obispo leproso* (Madrid:

Ediciones de la Torre, 1984). See *30*.

32. L. J. Woodward, 'Les Images et leur fonction dans *Nuestro Padre San Daniel*', *Bulletin Hispanique*, 56 (1954), 110–32. A pioneering essay on the symbolic function of imagery which opened the way to a revaluation of Miró as novelist.

ADDENDA

While the manuscript of this Guide was with the editors, the following important items, which I have regrettably been unable to take into account, became available:

33. Biblioteca Gabriel Miró, *Catálogo de los fondos de la biblioteca personal de Gabriel Miró* (Alicante: Caja de Ahorros del Mediterráneo, 1992). An essential research tool. An introduction by Ian Macdonald sheds further light on Miró's use of literary sources.

34. James H. Hoddie, *Unidad y universalidad en la ficción modernista de Gabriel Miró* (Madrid: Orígenes, 1992). Contains two interesting though diffuse essays on the Oleza novels. The first suggests that the many parallel situations reveal the quest for thematic unity, while the second argues that there is a shift from psychological terror to Christian compassion symbolised in the eyes and looks of images and characters.

35. F. Márquez Villanueva, 'Las tres lepras de *El obispo leproso*', in *La esfinge mironiana y otros estudios sobre Gabriel Miró* (Alicante: Instituto de Cultura Juan Gil Albert, 1990), pp.97–128. A brilliantly suggestive essay in which the author, building on an insight of Ricardo Gullón (*9*), uses the abundance of dermal motifs and dermatological allusions in the novel to argue that leprosy exists on three levels, physical, metaphorical and diegetic.

36. Manuel Ruiz-Funes, Introduction to his edition of *El obispo leproso* (Madrid: Ediciones Cátedra, 1989). The sequel to *29*. Important for both the introduction and the notes.

37. Rosario Martínez Galán, *Arte y técnica en la narrativa de Gabriel Miró* (Càdiz: Universidad de Càdiz, 1990). A laboured analysis of the Oleza novels employing a pseudo-scientific methodology that furnishes isolated insights but proves ultimately unrewarding.

As this Guide goes to press, a new and important edition of the Oleza novels by two leading Miró specialists, Edmund L. King and Ian R. Macdonald, has been announced by the Generalitat Valenciana.

CRITICAL GUIDES TO SPANISH TEXTS

Edited by
J.E. Varey, A.D. Deyermond and C. Davies

CRITICAL GUIDES TO SPANISH TEXTS

Edited by
J.E. Varey, A.D. Deyermond and C. Davies